DATE			

Explaining Human Action

Explaining Human Action

Kathleen Lennon

OPEN 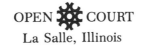 COURT
La Salle, Illinois

OPEN COURT and the above logo are registered in the
U.S. Patent and Trademark Office.

Published by arrangement with Gerald Duckworth & Co.
Ltd., London.

©1990 by Kathleen Lennon

Printed and bound in the United States of America.

Library of Congress Cataloging-in-Publication Data

Lennon, Kathleen.
  Explaining human action / Kathleen Lennon.
    p.   cm.
  Includes bibliographical references and index.
  ISBN 0-8126-9134-2. — ISBN 0-8126-9135-0 (pbk.)
  1. Motivation.   2. Intention.   3. Explanation.
4. Reductionism.   5. Functionalism (Psychology)
6. Science and psychology.
I. Title.
BF503.L45   1990
128′.4—dc20   90–38139
                                                CIP

Contents

Contents

7. Postscript: Individualism and Intentional Explanation

Acknowledgments

I am indebted to: St. Anne's College, Oxford, and especially Gabriele Taylor for providing the opportunity, many years ago, for me to re-enter philosophy; David Pears and the late John Mackie for rigorous criticism of my early research; Ismay Barwell, David Charles and Paul Gilbert for long hours of conversation on these matters over many years; my students at Hull; members of my household for comfort and support; my friends and political comrades (without whom this book might have been written more quickly, but from a life much more blinkered).

FOR THOSE PEOPLE WHO WOULD
BE PHILOSOPHERS GIVEN THE CHANCE

Preface

The term 'folk-psychology' is current as a way of referring to those of our everyday descriptions and explanations of people (and at least some animals), which involve attributing to them intentional states and explaining their actions by means of their reasons. The associations which the term carries can be misleading. They suggest that such psychological explanations are to be linked with those in everyday weather-lore or herbal medicine (in themselves dismissed too swiftly!) reflecting a set of beliefs, maybe useful, but unscientific, waiting to be replaced by a genuinely scientific account of human nature and behaviour. This scientific account is envisaged as employing a non-intentional, functional or physical vocabulary which will mesh comfortably with a materialist view of reality. It is just such a suggestion which this book aims to resist.

Reason-giving explanations form the basis of our everyday interaction with other people. They provide a model of understanding which is fundamental to both our view of ourselves and our view of others. We regard one another as 'rational purposive creatures, fitting our beliefs to the world as we perceive it and seeking to obtain what we desire in the light of them'.[1] To reject such a model of understanding ourselves seems scarcely intelligible, indeed self-defeating. Moreover the degree of

[1] James Hopkins, 'Introduction', Hopkins 1982.

11

success of inter-actions based on such a model, from time immemorial, requires us to take reason-giving explanations seriously as genuine and reputable accounts of how we come to behave as we do. As a consequence I shall accept that the presuppositions on which such explanations rest are likely to be true, and provide an instructive insight into our mode of responding to our environment. The strategy of this book is therefore to spell out the nature of these explanations, and to articulate and defend their presuppositions, in a way that provides a coherent theoretical framework for the explanation of action.

In Chapters One and Two the structure of reason-giving explanations is articulated as resting on the intentional content of our psychological states. It is argued that the commonsense psychology reflected in such explanations has the status of a causal explanatory theory; for it employs a system of conceptualisation of reality which generates laws and leads to successful predictions and retrodictions. The key point made in these chapters is that the causal explanatory connections expressed by our intentional explanations are *dependent on* the rationalising relations which make reason-giving links distinctive. At the psychological level, then, our causal explanatory laws rest on intentional modes of description.

Adopting such a view of our intentional level of description and explanation, has several important consequences explored in Chapters Three to Six. It does not rule out materialism. What is ruled out is the *reduction* of psychological laws or the intentional kinds they relate to those couched in physicalist or non-intentional functionalist terms. Intentional descriptions turn out to be indispensable modes of characterising aspects of reality, and capturing law-like connections

12

between them, which purely physical descriptions could not capture. Such anti-reductionism is shown to be compatible with both materialism and explanatory physicalism.

Chapter Seven rejects the suggestion that a causal explanatory view of intentional explanation requires an individualist account of the determinants of explanatory intentional content.

The position articulated in this book occupies a middle ground between opposing views which in much of the contemporary literature are regarded as exclusive.[1] Contemporary writers who adopt a causal explanatory view of psychological explanation, and with it a realist view of the mental, regard its reconciliation with materialism as requiring a functionalist reduction of intentional descriptions, or those elements of them relevant to causal explanations.[2] However, those who reject such functionalist reductions characteristically adopt a non-causal explanatory view of intentional explanation.[3] They see the irreducibility concerned as requiring that making sense of people's behaviour involves a different kind of explanation, occupying a different explanatory space from that offered in science. One of the purposes of this book is to illustrate the possibility of a unified theory combining those elements, previously regarded as in opposition.

Clearly the framework adopted here has consequences for the human sciences. First, it reconciles the humanist demand that we explain our behaviour in a way that reflects the meaning we ourselves attach to it, with the

[1] Loar, Introduction, 1981.

[2] Loar 1981; Fodor 1980, 1985; Field 1978.

[3] Davidson 1980; McDowell 1978, 1985; Putnam 1978 and 'Computational psychology and interpretation theory', in Putnam 1983.

requirement that if we are engaged in science we must search for causal regularities. Secondly, however, it upsets a picture of the unity of science which sees the laws of each distinctive level of taxonomy as ultimately reducible to those of physics. This framework gives human sciences a place which is both scientific and autonomous, without at any stage denying the truth of materialism.

CHAPTER ONE

Reason-giving Explanations

1. Introducing intentional acts

Consider two cases of my leg moving upwards: (1) My knee is hit by a hammer, on a particular point which produces the movement of my leg by means of a reflex. In giving an account of this movement I myself am really in no better a position than, for example, the person who hit me with the hammer. How fully either of us can explain it depends on how much biological knowledge we have. (2) My knee is hit, but not on the spot which initiates the reflex response. I jerk my leg upwards to kick the person who hit me. This is an instance of that area of my behaviour which is distinguished from the reflex and involuntary and designated action. My position with regard to my actions is considered to be quite different from my position with regard to my involuntary and reflex movements. I am in some way held responsible for them and can be asked to give an account of why I performed them. It is with explanation of human behaviour of this second type, commonly termed intentional action, that this book will be primarily concerned. Such behaviour is not restricted to human beings. Many animals can also act in this way, but it is in human beings that such action takes its most complex form. There does not appear to be a special problem about behaviour of the first kind. We do not expect its explanation to differ fundamentally from that offered for other natural phenomena – for example, one billiard ball hitting another and causing it to move. That is, we are quite happy to accept the view that such behaviour will be explicable by reference to antecedent causes and will be governed by some scientific law valid for all relevantly similar sequences. In the second kind of case, however, the search for intelligibility appears to take a different form. Here we seem concerned to discover how the agent regarded the action and the circumstances in which it occurred. Crucially we are seeking to understand the point or purpose of the activity from the agent's point of view.

In the case of intentional action the behaviour which ensues must correspond to that which the agent intended to perform. I intended *to kick my assailant* and *kicked my assailant*.[1] One way to explain my behaviour is to point to the corresponding intention. Such an explanation may appear trivial, but it is not so. First, it indicates that the action performed was intentional, and moreover in what

[1] It might be suggested that the agent's action need not, as a matter of fact, correspond to her intention, but must rather be believed by her to do so. I might intend to attract someone's attention and make certain movements which I take to be doing so, and fail. Yet I might not be able to articulate some alternative description of these movements, such that I could avow an intention to perform movements of that kind. Even in such cases, however, the movements actually produced must correspond to what the agent had 'in mind', even if she is unable to articulate a correct description of them. An agent can intend to perform an act of a certain kind without being able linguistically to characterise the kind, as would be expected given that animals and very young children perform intentional acts. We do, however, need to distinguish intentional acts from cases where the agent takes herself to be moving her arm, and in fact moves her leg. (She may even be in a situation where the only feedback available to her suggests that she has been successful.) In such cases no intentional act is performed.

respects it was intentional. There are many ways we might characterise an agent's sequence of behaviour, but only some of these will reflect the agent's actual intentions in acting. Frequently, however, the behaviour intentionally performed has some further point or purpose, and in seeking to understand it we also need to know what led the agent to form the intention to act as she did. Maybe in the above case I was seeking to teach my assailant a lesson.

When we seek the further point or purpose in our agent's action we are seeking the agent's reasons for intending and acting as she does. Classically an agent has a reason for performing a certain kind of action when she has (a) a 'pro-attitude' towards some end or objective, and (b) a belief that an action of that kind will promote this end. The term 'pro-attitude' derives from Donald Davidson. It includes:

> desires, wantings, urges, promptings, and a great variety of moral views, aesthetic principles, economic prejudices, social conventions, and public and private goals and values in so far as these can be interpreted as attitudes of an agent directed toward actions of a certain kind. The word 'attitude' does yeoman service here, for it must cover not only permanent character traits that show themselves in a lifetime of behaviour, like love of children or a taste for loud company, but also the most passing fancy that prompts a unique action like a sudden desire to touch a woman's elbow.[1]

As has become common, I will frequently use 'desire' as a generic term for such pro-attitudes.

When we wish to explain an agent's actions by citing

[1] See Davidson, 'Actions, reasons and causes', in Davidson 1980, 4. The pro-attitudes required to provide reasons for actions can, of course, include evaluative beliefs. Nothing in the characterisation given is meant to exclude the suggestion that these might be

17

reasons, the reasons concerned have to be *her* reasons. We say that there is *a* reason for an agent to perform an action (maybe take up regular exercise) when, as a matter of fact, doing that would promote something conducive to her well-being (maybe good health), or bring about some other good. Such reasons, however, can play no role in explaining the agent's actual behaviour, unless the agent comes to recognise them as such. The agent's own view of the situation is what must provide the reasons by reference to which her action is explained. It is suggested, then, that whenever an agent acts intentionally she has a reason for so acting. We understand the action when we have access to the appropriate beliefs and desires which provide the agent's reasons for her intending, and thereby acting, as she does.

Not all behaviour which we may wish to term intentional action is behaviour which we can explain in terms of some further purpose or goal of the agent. I may kick my assailant just because I feel like kicking her, not to teach her a lesson, or stop her hitting out again. Such cases are, however, cases where the agent has a minimal reason for acting, for we understand her action when we understand that she desired to perform an action of just this kind. Even though the content of the agent's desire and intention may appear to be the same here (I desire to kick my assailant and intend to do so) it is appropriate to distinguish the two states. An agent can have a number of desires, which conflict with each other, and cannot be co-satisfied, without any failure of rationality. When she intends to act, however, such a conflict has been resolved in favour of a given course of action. If an agent is able to

---

considered appropriate, and in part cognitive, responses to objective features of the world.

act on her intention she will, given that she believes the moment for action has arrived. A conflict in intentions would therefore mean an incoherent conflict of such dispositions. Intentions, moreover, require a component of belief.[1] To intend to do A the agent must believe there is some chance of her doing A as a result of her intentions. Moreover (as has been emphasised by Bratman)[2] intentions play a role in co-ordinating our future plans, which need to be both internally consistent and consistent with our beliefs about the future. In all these respects intentions are distinct from mere wants.

Whenever an agent acts intentionally, then, her action must correspond to her intention, and this intention must be reason-based, in the sense that there is some desire which supports it, even if the desire is simply to perform an action of that kind.

2. The reason-giving relation

In order to give an account of the explanation of those areas of human behaviour which count as purposive or intentional acts we therefore need an account of the nature of reason-giving explanations. This will consist of two components: (1) An account of the *reason-giving relation*, i.e. the connections between beliefs, desires, intentions and actions in virtue of which such intentional states provide reasons for acting; (2) An account of the relation between reason-giving states and actions when such states *explain why* the agent acted as she did. (1) and (2) are not equivalent. For we have reasons to do many things we don't do, and reasons for doing many of

---

[1] For the relation of intention and belief, see Grice 1971; Davidson, 'Intending', in Davidson 1980; Pears 1985; Charles 1984c.
[2] Bratman 1984 and 1985.

the things we do which are not the reasons for which we act. I shall begin with (1).

The psychological states which give an agent reasons for acting – broadly beliefs, desires and intentions – are all intentional states. Intentional states are individuated by what kind of state they are, e.g. as a desire, belief, intention, hope, wish or fear, but also by means of the sentence or proposition which in their description follows the *that* clause, e.g. a belief that the house is dark, a desire that I remain unharmed, a fear that the darkness will engulf me, an intention that I should remain stoical. With regard to such states we need to use a proposition or sentence[1] to give their content. Without specifying their content we fail to individuate them. What often seems paradoxical is that the sentences which we use to specify the intentional contents of our intentional states are sentences which are otherwise used to describe actual or possible states of affairs in the world: the house being dark, my remaining unharmed, the darkness engulfing me, my remaining stoical.

The phenomenon of intentional content is one to which I shall give more extended treatment later. It is important, however, to note at this point that it is on just these apparently paradoxical features that the special character of intentional explanation rests. For, as pointed out above, what an agent does intentionally must match or correspond with what she intends to do, and what this means is that the same sentence can be used to describe the action produced as is used to characterise

---

[1] The contents of some intentional states seem to be given not by whole sentences, but by sub-sentential components, e.g. I want a Burmese kitten. For present purposes I shall assume that the contents of those intentional states which give us reasons for acting, if fully spelt out, could be characterised by means of a sentence, e.g. I want it to be the case that I own a Burmese kitten.

the content of the agent's intention. The intentional
content of our intentional states is that feature on which
their reason-giving links to each other and to the agent's
behaviour depend.

There is a long tradition which emphasises that the
reason-giving relation is a logical or conceptual one, and
one way of bringing out the nature of the conceptual link
is by the construction of *reasoning* linking an agent's
reason-giving states with those actions for which they
provide reasons. Donald Davidson[1] puts the matter thus:

> If someone acts with an intention then he must have
> attitudes and beliefs, from which had he been aware of
> them and had the time, he could have reasoned that his
> action was desirable ... If we can characterise the
> reasoning that would serve, we will, in effect have
> described the logical relations between descriptions of
> beliefs and desires, and the description of the action,
> when the former gives the reasons with which the latter
> was performed. We are to imagine, then, that the agent's
> beliefs and desires provide him with the premises of an
> argument.

The possibility of constructing reasoning linking intentional states with each other and with behaviour does not
presuppose that whenever an agent acts for reasons she
consciously rehearses the pattern of argument which we
may construct. The reasoning is, however, derived from
the intentional contents of her intentional states. It
makes explicit certain conceptual connections between
the contents of such states and the description of the
action for which they provide reasons. These are just the
links which are constitutive of the reason-giving relation.

Before tackling the form of practical reasoning directly
it is worth attending to theoretical reasoning, that

[1] Davidson 1980, 85-6.

illustrative of the reason-giving relation between beliefs, in the hope of bringing out the nature of reasons for action by both comparison and contrast. Where a believer has reasons for her belief, the premises of the reconstructed argument are provided by the intentional contents of reason-providing beliefs. Such premises must support a conclusion, either inductively or deductively, which forms the intentional content of the belief for which they form a reason. For example, I believe that my grandmother is sitting in her garden now, and my reasons are (1) my grandmother always (or usually) sits in her garden after lunch, if the sun is shining. (2) The sun is shining, and it is just after lunch. According to the form of the first premise this argument is valid either deductively or inductively. If the agent accepts the premises, she has a reason to accept the conclusion. It is not difficult to see why, in the case of belief, the reason-giving relation consists of deductive or inductive support. To believe a proposition is to accept it as true. So it is relative to the objective of reaching truths that the standards of rationality are set for belief. When we are reconstructing the reason-giving link we are looking for a relationship between the premises and the conclusion of the argument which makes it rational for someone who accepts the premises to accept the conclusion. Given the nature of belief, therefore, the relationship in the case of theoretical reasoning must be such that the truth of the premises makes likely (or certain) the truth of the conclusion.

In the case of practical reasoning philosophers have also sought to articulate the nature of the reason-giving link by displaying the relationship between the premises and the conclusion of an argument, in such a way that it is rational for someone who accepts the premises to accept the conclusion. However, in the case of reasons for action the premises will be provided by desires as well as beliefs, for desires are among the intentional states which provide us with reasons for acting. Moreover the conclusion of the reasoning in the practical case must be one whose acceptance by the agent involves some direct link to action. We can attend to this latter point directly. Some writers have suggested that an agent's intentional act can be represented as the acceptance of a proposition. But this seems wrong. An action is not a propositional attitude, though forming an intention to perform one is. (As David Pears puts it, an action is a contribution to the world, not a picture of it.)[1] Here it will be assumed that the aim of practical reasoning is to reach a conclusion whose acceptance constitutes the formation of an intention to act. The ensuing action is thereby rationalised, if it corresponds to the intention.

Suppose someone has just put an advertisement in the evening paper, 'Wanted: one Burmese kitten', and her reasons are that she wants to own a Burmese kitten and she believes that putting an advertisement in the paper will help to achieve this. If we take the intentional content of the desire to be captured by the proposition which describes the state of affairs which the agent wishes to bring into existence, and attempt to construct an argument from the contents of the belief and desire forming the reasons, in a way that apparently parallels the belief case, we get the following two premises: (1) I come to own a Burmese kitten, (2) placing an advertisement in the paper will help bring it about that I own a Burmese kitten. However, as Davidson notes,[2] nothing follows from (1) and (2) thus expressed concerning what I shall or should do. What is required is that we feed into the propositional expression of desire

[1] Pears 1984, 156-7.
[2] Davidson 1980, 86.

23

(or other pro-attitude) that it is a content whose acceptance constitutes desire and not belief. In such a way we might hope to derive a conclusion whose acceptance would be practical in outcome. Davidson's own suggestion is that the contents of desires find expression in the proposition that the goal concerned is desirable. This would render the practical reasoning in the case of our cat lover as follows:

P_1 My owning a Burmese kitten is desirable.

P_2 Putting an advertisement in the paper will help bring it about that I own a Burmese kitten.

C Putting an advertisement in the paper is desirable.

To accept the first premise would be to desire to own such a kitten, to accept the second to have a belief, and to accept the conclusion to form a *derived desire* in favour of the course of action.

Such an argument captures at least part of the reason-giving connections in the practical case. It is valid, however, neither inductively nor deductively,[1] so how can it be defended as a process of reasoning? The practical argument, thus formalised, shares two important features with theoretical reasoning: (a) It consists of a set of premises and a conclusion, such that if an agent

---

[1] Davidson's initial characterisation of the practical argument in 'Intending' appears to give it a deductive or inductive nature: P_1: Any action of improving the stew is good (desirable); P_2: Adding sage will (or probably will) improve the stew; C: Adding sage will (or probably will) be good (desirable). However, in expressing the content of desire in the form that any actions which promote the object of desire are themselves desirable, Davidson is relying on the principle of rationality governing desire which I make explicit.

24

accepts the premises and is rational she will accept the conclusion (see below). (b) The rationality of such acceptance is a consequence of conceptual links between the propositions forming the premises and conclusions.

What has to be explained is why a rational agent accepting the premises of a practical argument would also accept the conclusion. Processes of reasoning establish what a reasoner who accepts the premises needs also to accept if she is not to be, in some sense, self-defeating. In the case of theoretical reasoning we explained this by the claim that beliefs had the objective of truth. The relation between premises and conclusion in the theoretical case, therefore, concerned what, if the premises were true, was also necessarily or probably true. The matter is different when we are concerned with desires. In contrast to belief we might say that the objective of desires is their own satisfaction.[1] To desire some state of affairs is to aim to make it true. What reasoning involving desires therefore needs to establish is what else an agent needs to make true, if the state of affairs characterised in the first premise is to be made true. It is from a recognition of this distinctive feature of desire that the claim is made that 'she who desires the end must desire the means'.[2]

The strength of the reasoning displayed by the practical argument can vary. If the second premise states a condition necessary and sufficient for the achievement of the agent's goal, the agent has the strongest reason for accepting the conclusion. If it states only possible means,

---

[1] See Charles 1982/3, 1984c.

[2] Must I desire the poisoned chocolate if I recognise that it would satisfy my craving for sugar? Desires, we must remember, only dispose us to act, other things being equal, and what might be rational from the standpoint of one desire might not be so from the standpoint of the agent overall (see below).

the support for the conclusion is correspondingly diluted. There is a clear analogy here with deductive and inductive support in the case of theoretical reasoning.

Can the claims that the objective of belief is truth, and that of desire satisfaction be unpacked in a less metaphorical way? For it is here that our concepts of rational support have been grounded. Such teleological claims result from attention to the place played by belief and desire in our overall theory explaining the behaviour of intentional agents. These states are individuated by their role in mediating an agent's response to her environment (see below, especially Chapters Three and Seven). Philip Pettit has recently pointed out that when we offer intentional explanations we are explaining systems which have achieved 'certain environmental equilibrium'. The focus of such explanations is 'on the system considered in environmental integration'.[1] It is in the context of this explanatory goal that the distinct roles of different intentional states are located. As a crude approximation a state counts as a belief if its conditional dispositional role shows sensitivity to how things are in the world, and the pattern of internal transformations it produces are truth-preserving so that the resultant states guiding an agent's behaviour will also be sensitive to how things are. A state counts as a desire if it is a conditional disposition to produce behaviour likely to satisfy the desire, other things being equal. It is in the light of such constitutive roles that the 'objectives' of belief and desire are fixed, and from these the pattern of rational transformations between them. It is therefore partially constitutive of each of these intentional states that they yield other intentional states, for which they provide reasons. But there is some

[1] P. Pettit, 'Broad-minded explanation and psychology', in McDowell & Pettit 1986.

26

room for slack, some room for irrationality. An agent can have some irrational beliefs and desires, which are none the less recognisably beliefs and desires. This is possible, however, only so far as the overall function of such states are recognisably truth-promoting or satisfaction-promoting; and this, of course, sets limits on the extent to which such irrationality is possible.

How far have we got with the project of spelling out what the connection between desires/beliefs/intentions and action consists in when the intentional states provide a reason for the action? It has been claimed that, where an agent has a reason for acting, it is possible to construct a practical argument from her desires and beliefs to a conclusion whose acceptance would constitute a derived desire in favour of the action concerned. This may not appear sufficient, however, for as we noted above, a desire to perform a course of action is not yet an intention to perform it. We therefore need to consider whether the moves from such derived desires to the formation of an intention can be represented in a reason-giving way, that is as a move which under certain conditions it is rational for the agent to make. We cannot simply say that it is rational to form an intention to do A, given a derived desire in favour of A. It is true that the formation of an intention is a necessary step in the satisfaction of the desire, and therefore something for which there is a reason from the standpoint of that desire; but from the agent's point of view overall it may well not be rational to satisfy certain desires. This, of course, results from the fact that the satisfaction of one goal may be inconsistent with the achievement of others which are more important to the agent. It would not be rational to satisfy my desire for something sweet by eating poisoned chocolate. It is only in situations where the agent has no conflicting goals that the move from the

27

derived desire to intention is unproblematically a rational one.

The rationality of the move from a derived desire to the formation of an intention needs to take account of the total set of objectives which the agent has, and how, from her viewpoint, they add up one against the other. If such a choice is reason-based there will be some means of assessing the conflicting goals, by reference to which it can be judged more rational to pursue one rather than the other. Moreover if we maintain our stance of seeking rationality from the agent's viewpoint, the grounds of the comparison must be an assignment of priorities which the agent accepts and in the light of which she requires her decisions to be made.

Again there are both similarities and differences with the theoretical case. An agent may hold beliefs which provide inductive support for conflicting conclusions. Given that the sky is red she has reason to believe it will stay fine. Given that the barometer is falling she has reason to believe it will rain.[1] In such cases if she is to have a reason for accepting one of these conclusions rather than another she must have a way of comparing the competing evidence in a way that will yield one outcome as best supported overall. There is however a crucial difference from the practical·case. When we are comparing theoretical reasons, the overall objective in regard to which alternative evidence is to be compared is given by the nature of belief itself. We require a method of comparison most likely to yield true beliefs. It does not seem possible, however, to derive from the nature of desire some overall objective in the light of which all our goals should be compared and a judgment reached that it is more rational to pursue one goal than another. It

[1] See Davidson, 'How is weakness of will possible?' for such analogies with probablistic reasoning, in Davidson 1980.

28

therefore seems up to each agent to determine the criteria in terms of which she wishes her decisions to be made. These criteria may be complex. They may vary from agent to agent, and within one agent at different times.

How is this to be reflected in the reasoning we reconstruct to characterise the rationalising links between desires/beliefs and intentions? One question is how the agent's *intention* is to be represented. We require a content whose acceptance by the agent commits her to acting, but which is linked to earlier stages in the practical reasoning, and can be seen to be supported by them. Davidson suggests that intentions find expression in 'general-purpose'[1] evaluative judgments. In 'How is weakness of will possible?' the judgment concerned is that *A is better than B*, where A is the act intended and B the alternative (or set of alternatives). Such a judgment points forward to action, for where an agent accepts it and believes herself free to do either A or B, she will intentionally do A if she does either A or B intentionally.[2] It also points backwards to the agent's reasoning in terms of which A rather than B is judged to satisfy the agent's preferred criterion of choice.

Such an identification of intentions with evaluations,

[1] Reply to Peacocke in Vermazen & Hintikka 1985, 210/11: 'It is difficult to think of a way to represent the nature of practical reasoning without introducing a general-purpose evaluative word, for the following reason. Suppose we keep our rich array of evaluative words in our regimented notation. Then we will have "pf" statements of many kinds, to express our reasons for holding some things to be obligatory, other things desirable, still further things good, and so forth. But now all these considerations are relevant to the question whether to perform a given action (or try to). We need a word or phrase to use in sentences that express an intention − a word or phrase that will distinguish such sentences from sentences that simply express a belief.'

[2] Davidson 1980, 23.

however, seems misplaced. An agent can form an intention to act without accepting such a value judgment. David Pears[1] gives an example in which we can take either red and green pills for our pains, but not both, and both are equally effective. We have to *pick* which pills to take, without considering picking those pills to be in any sense better than the alternative. Other examples concern occasions when we are only too painfully aware that we lack the crucial information that would enable us to judge what course of action is all-out best (will my attacker react to my anger with fear or added rage?).[2] In cases where different considerations support each alternative, it sometimes is not possible to arbitrate between the reasons and reach a conclusion that one course of action is best (should I save the child or the adult with my dose of penicillin?) In all these cases we appear to form intentions without judging that the act intended is the best one to perform. Most problematic for the suggested identification of intentions and evaluations are cases of *acrasia*, or weakness of will. We sometimes knowingly and fully intentionally act against what we judge to be the better course of action. The following would be an example. Someone is sitting up late in order to finish a paper for the next day. She wants a glass of port because she believes it will cheer her up, but she also wants to finish her paper and believes that the port will make this difficult. She considers a while, and forms a judgment that it would be better to do without the drink. Then she intentionally pours the port and drinks it down.[3]

[1] D. Pears in conversation.

[2] Bratman 1979.

[3] Davidson, of course, recognises the difficulty posed by cases of *acrasia*. His suggestion in 'How is weakness of will possible?' (Davidson 1980) attempts to overcome it by attributing to the acratic

1. Reason-giving Explanations

If we reject the identification of an intention with a comparative evaluation in favour of the action chosen, we still need to recognise that such evaluations provide the best reasons for intentions, and thereby for actions. Choices formed against them, as in the acratic case, are paradigmatically irrational. Why is this? Where an agent has a basic or derived desire to do A she has a reason for intending to do A. The reason-giving link here derives from the nature of desire and the objective of satisfaction. Intending and acting are required for the desire to be satisfied. What the agent does not have, on the basis of such a desire, is a reason for intending to do A rather than any of the alternatives open to her. Thus far the objective of desire has been given as satisfaction, but this is not quite accurate. In having desires I am committed to pursuing their satisfaction only conditionally, only if they do not conflict with other goals of mine. The case is different when I engage in deliberation, to compare the alternatives in front of me, and reach a conclusion concerning which one it is best to pursue. Here my commitment to the principles which guide that deliberation is stronger than that of mere desire. I don't simply want my choices to be made a certain way. I have accepted that they are to be made in such a way, without the added condition that other things must be equal. Choice-giving preferences have the goal of satisfaction *per se*, and not conditionally. It is rational for me to form my intention on the basis of such deliberations, for this is what is required to complete the commitment which I make when weighing the alternatives in the light of my preferred criterion of choice.

---

agent *two* general purpose evaluations, one *prima facie*, conditional on the evidence considered, opposing the act taken; the other all-out and in favour of the acratic act. For criticism of this view see Grice & Baker 1985; Barwell & Lennon 1982/3; and Hurley 1985/6.

The evaluations which guide our deliberations are therefore distinctive intentional states, and to qualify as such states must display the appropriate links to intentions and actions which allow their individuating objective to be identified. As was the case with beliefs and desires, however, for a state to count as an evaluation it does not always need to yield successfully the intention which it rationally requires. We are not perfectly rational. But the extent of the irrationality is curtailed. Our intentional states must display sufficient of the appropriate links with each other to enable us to identify their distinctive objectives, and thereby classify them as desires, beliefs or evaluations at all.

A perfectly rational intention, then, expressible perhaps, as 'A is to be done', will be one supported by a comparative evaluation, 'It is better to do A than the alternatives.' Such an evaluation will be reached by comparing the alternatives in the light of the agent's preferred criterion of choice. Where such an evaluation is accepted by the agent she is said, traditionally, to have a sufficient reason for intending and thereby acting. Our examples have made clear however that intentions are frequently formed in the absence of such sufficient reasons; or even directly in the face of opposing reasons. In such cases the agent's intention and action is not entirely without reason. The course of action will be recognised to promote the satisfaction of some desire, and this provides *a* reason for it; even if not a sufficient one.

To summarise. The concern of this section has been to articulate what the reason-giving relation consists in when an agent has a reason for acting in a certain way. This articulation proceeded by constructing practical reasoning, linking the agent's intentional states. Such reasoning leads to a conclusion whose acceptance by the agent constitutes an intention to act. The construction of such reasoning, and therefore the reason-giving link itself, depends on broadly conceptual links between the intentional contents of the intentional states. Reason-giving links are therefore constituted out of links between these intentional contents. Practical reasoning is distinct from theoretical reasoning, but shares the feature that acceptance of the premises supports the acceptance of the conclusion, if the agent is not to be in some sense self-defeating. The principles of rational acceptance in each case are determined in relation to the overall objectives of beliefs, desires and choice-guiding preferences. The reason-giving relation admits of degree. In the case of reasons for belief the support provided can vary from deductive entailment to some inductive probability. In the case of reasons for acting (via reasons for intending), the support can vary from a sufficient reason constituted by the agent's all-out evaluation in favour of the action, to a minimal reason favouring the action from the viewpoint of a single goal, and there will be many stages in between. The beliefs and actions of an agent can therefore display degrees of rationality. It is also possible for an agent to form irrational beliefs/desires/intentions, but the extent of such irrationality is restricted on pain of our being able to individuate such intentional states at all.

3. Explaining with reasons

The reason-giving link is not a purely descriptive one. Giving reasons is a *justificatory* and *explanatory* activity. It is to these aspects of reason-giving that we should now turn. When we put forward an agent's reasons for believing or acting we are showing that the belief or action was to some degree appropriate, at least from the agent's own point of view. The notion of appropriateness here is a normative one, as is the notion of rationality itself. To believe or act irrationally is to be subject to criticism. The appropriateness of the belief/action for which the agent has reasons derives from the fact that it is rationally required by further intentional states which she has (at least when we confine ourselves to internal rationality).[1] The construction of theoretical and practical reasoning, the possibility of which is constitutive of the reason-giving relation, makes explicit such requirements. The normative nature of reason-giving links is not such as to render them less factual. It is a matter of fact whether or not reason-giving links hold between certain sets of intentional states. It is none the less the case that where such links hold the ensuing states can be seen to be justified. This is a process which admits of degrees. According to the tightness of connections articulated in the reasoning, the ensuing belief/action is displayed as being justified to a greater or lesser degree.

It was noted earlier that to give an account of reason-giving explanation we need to consider two questions: first the nature of the reason-giving link, and secondly the relation between reason-giving states and actions when such states explain why the agent acted as she did. When we turn to the second question the

[1] Our concern has been only internal rationality: that is, what it would be rational for an agent to believe or intend given other intentional states of hers. This is because the focus of attention is on explanation by reasons and such explanation proceeds via the agent's own intentional states. Where our primary purpose is justification, however, we employ notions of rationality in which the formation of intentional states, including emotional responses, are judged more or less rational, in terms of being appropriate to how the world really is or to the goals and objectives which agents should have. Such external criteria of rationality will not be discussed here.

1. Reason-giving Explanations

justificatory nature of the reason-giving relation is clearly pertinent. To show that a certain course of action was required in my lights to satisfy my goals is a central part of what makes that action intelligible. For some writers the justificatory and explanatory tasks of reason-giving simply coincide. To explain a belief/intention/action is to show that it was appropriate given the agent's other intentional states. On this account the manifestation of rationality is seen as carrying with it its own intelligibility, sufficient to explain the states or acts quite independently of questions regarding causal origin. Leibniz contrasted explanations in terms of reasons, 'final causes', which provided logically sufficient conditions for their explananda, with explanations of events given in terms of 'efficient causes', providing mechanically sufficient conditions for their effects.[1] For Leibniz the logically sufficient condition for action was provided by the agent's judgment that it was the best thing to do. It was argued above, however, that it is possible for an agent to act intentionally, and for a reason, without such a judgment. If this point is accepted, within a model which equates explanation and justification, actions which are not based on comparative evaluations will be less intelligible. The greater the degree of rationality we can detect, the more intelligible the sequence will be. Where there is a breakdown in rationality as in cases of *acrasia*, or beliefs based on wishful thinking or self-deception, there is a corresponding breakdown in our ability to make the action/belief intelligible. Where we can detect no reason-giving links at all, we can no longer make the behaviour intelligible as human action and revert to a mechanistic, causal model to explain the movement.[2]

[1] Leibniz in *The Leibniz-Clark Correspondence*. This position is discussed in Barwell & Lennon 1982/3.

[2] Such a picture is suggested in Dennett, 'Intentional systems' and

There are, however, problems with simply equating explanation and justification. On such an account a valid explanation could be provided by any of the agent's intentional states linked to the action/belief in a reason-giving way. But this is clearly not the case. I may have beliefs from which your innocence could be deduced but none the less come to believe you are innocent because you have blue eyes. I may have intentional states which give me altruistic reasons for giving to charity but none the less contribute out of a desire to earn someone's good opinion. In both these cases, although my belief could be shown to be rational in the light of other beliefs, and my action in the light of my altruistic states, neither of these rationalising links would form part of a valid explanation of the phenomena concerned. There are moreover further problems which deserve attention. On the account being considered we have the best explanation in cases where the action/belief is shown to be maximally rational. For action this is when the agent forms a best judgment in favour of the action. Such a judgment must therefore be sufficient to explain actions based on it, and in its absence any action is correspondingly less intelligible. But consider two versions of our midnight drinker story, maybe myself on two different nights. One night I drink the port. The next night I abstain. Each night my beliefs and desires are the same, and so the reasons both for and against the drinking remain the same. Each night I think it better to abstain. Yet only on one night do I abstain. On the occasion on which I do as I think best it is clear that, from my own point of view, I have sufficient reason for what I do. My action can be explained by pointing to the reasons which make it the most rational course to adopt. There is

---

'Mechanism and responsibility', in Dennett 1979.

a problem, however, for exactly the same reasoning is available when I take the drink and therefore fail to do what is best. What this points to is this. The mere availability of reasoning, however good, in favour of an action cannot in itself be sufficient to explain why it occurred. For an agent may have reasons just as good on another occasion and fail to act. Where pointing to an agent's reasons does explain an action, there must be something more that can be said. Conversely, but connectedly, my weakness on one night may be quite explicable. I may be more tired or more depressed on that occasion, although that does not alter my judgment concerning what it would be best to do.

If we resist the equation of the justificatory and explanatory work of reason-giving, we must look for a connection between reasons and action/belief in cases where those reasons genuinely explain, which is absent in cases of mere rationalisations, a connection which is present when I act on my best judgment and not when I resist it. Classically, of course, the connection that has been suggested here is that of causality. In cases of genuine explanation the reason-providing intentional states cause the beliefs/actions for which they also provide reasons. This will be the view adopted in this book, and much of the next chapter is taken up with a defence of it. More needs to be said, however, if such a view is not to leave us with a picture in which reason-giving explanations perform two quite disconnected tasks: namely, show an action/belief to be rational and point to its causes. To avoid such a picture I shall be giving an exposition and defence of the claim that reason-giving explanations are a sub-species of causal explanations in which the causal links are dependent on the reason-giving ones. What this claim requires can be made clearer by considering the following example.

Imagine that a hypnotist sets up a mechanism such that regardless of the content of my next belief *it* will produce a further belief with the content that there are six apples on the table. The hypnotist then induces in me a belief which happens to have as its content that there are two groups of apples on the table, with three apples in each group. Here I would have ended up with the belief that there were six apples on the table, regardless of the content of the preceding belief which caused it. In such a situation it would be quite inappropriate to point to the reason-giving relation between the two beliefs, in explanation of the second. In this example the fact that the first belief provided a reason for the second is *causally irrelevant* to the fact that the agent came to adopt a second belief of that kind. (The concept of causal relevancy will be explicated in more detail in the following chapter.) Where we can legitimately point to an agent's reasons to explain a certain belief or action, then those features of the agent's intentional states which render the belief or action reasonable, i.e. those features which allow the construction of theoretical or practical reasoning, must be causally relevant in explaining how the agent came to believe or act in a way which they rationalised. One way of putting this requirement is as the demand that reason-giving states not only cause but *causally explain* their explananda.

This account yields the following model of the connection between the abstract structure of theoretical and practical reasoning and the process whereby an agent comes to hold a new belief or initiate an action, in cases where reasons are genuinely explanatory. An agent has certain intentional states (those which provide the premises of the argument). She goes through a process which results in her having further intentional states (those which provide the conclusion of the argument) and sometimes in initiating an action (of the kind described in the conclusion). In cases where the agent believes or acts for reasons this process is causally explained by the fact that the sequence of intentional states and the action/belief concerned are of such kinds that they can be linked by means of a theoretical or practical argument. Where this is so reconstructing the reasoning, whether or not the agent consciously rehearses it, makes explicit the characteristics on which the causal links depend. The causal links required here, however, do not depend solely on the reason-giving ones. Our discussion of *acrasia* made clear that where an agent has a reason for acting, even *a sufficient reason*, this *is not*, on its own *a causally sufficient condition* for action. The circumstances in which an agent's intentional states occur determine whether or not they will be causally sufficient to bring about an action of the kind rationalised. There will therefore be a difference in the circumstances of the weak-willed drinker and the rational abstainer, which serves to explain why in one case the agent's best judgment takes effect in action, and in the other not. Such differences, however, need not consist in differences in the intentional contents of their reason-giving states, and so the reasoning available to each of them may be parallel. What this shows is that the causal links between intentional states and actions are partially dependent on states of the agent which are not themselves intentional, and/or on features of their intentional states other than their intentional content. Within such a view it is possible for the irrational act to be fully explained, and in that sense fully intelligible, without being fully rational. It will be explained by invoking those circumstances which determine that the agent's acratic goal becomes effective in action, rather than her best judgment: maybe, in this case, a prevailing feeling of depression. This seems right. For we might perfectly understand how the midnight drinker came to be drinking the port, and if we knew her well might even have successfully predicted that her desire to be cheered up would prove stronger than her best judgment.[1]

What such cases force us to recognise is that for most of us it is not only in so far as a reason comes out best in terms of the reasoning that it can become operative. A fully rational agent (Aristotle's virtuous (wo)man?) will be one whose overall state is such that the fact that certain reasons are recognised by her to be rationally strongest will always be causally sufficient to determine choice in accordance with them. For the rest of us this is only true some of the time. The justificatory strength of our reasons and their causal strength can diverge. Even a weak-willed agent has a reason for acting, however, and what this means is that her reason-providing intentional states played an essential causal explanatory role in producing an action of just the kind for which they provided reasons. Such a claim is not undermined by the need for non-intentional conditions to ensure the causal effectiveness of these intentional states.

4. Conclusion

At the beginning of this chapter I drew a contrast between those areas of human behaviour for which explanations in terms of reasons were available and

[1] The acratic action can be fully explained, but none the less fewer of the causal explanatory links determining such behaviour depend on reason-giving links than is the case with the fully rational agent. The rational agent's choice between goals is determined by the fact that she has a *reason* to pursue one rather than the other. For the acratic agent the choice between goals is determined by factors which neither yield nor depend on such reason-giving links (e.g. a general feeling of depression).

1. Reason-giving Explanations

those areas of behaviour whose explanation was given in terms of causes. We now see that the contrast was drawn in the wrong way. I accepted that there were categories of human behaviour, namely intentional acts, which were made intelligible in a special sort of way, by being shown to be rational in the light of the agent's intentional states. Such intelligibility we have now seen is not in contra-distinction to causal explanation. It provides a particularly crucial sub-species of it, a sub-species in which causal links depend on rationalising ones. There is not a contrast here between empirical causal explanation, and explanation which depends on conceptual links. In the areas of human behaviour with which I have been concerned the causal links between the agent's intentional states and the agent's action depend on conceptual connections between the contents of such states and the description of the action. It is the consequences of this central fact regarding reason-giving explanations which will occupy the rest of this book.

41

CHAPTER TWO

Reason-giving Explanations as Causal Explanations: the Argument from Conditionals

1. Conditional claims implied by reason-giving explanations

In Chapter One I suggested that the explanatory force of reason-giving explanations can be most satisfactorily accommodated by regarding them as a special category of causal explanation. Where such explanations are appropriate, the fact that an agent had intentional states of a kind to rationalise a certain course of action causally explains the occurrence of an action of that kind. In this chapter I shall further defend and explicate this claim by a consideration of key conditionals which valid intentional explanations sustain.

Imagine that I am driving in Yugoslavia, heading for Dubrovnik, approaching a fork in the road. Given appropriate circumstances the following conditionals will be true of me. (i) If I believe the right fork leads to Dubrovnik I take the right fork. (ii) If I believe the left fork leads to Dubrovnik I take the left fork. These conditionals are true if my choice of route is to be explained by my desire to reach Dubrovnik and my beliefs concerning the road that will take me there. We can express the general form of such conditionals thus:

(1) Given C, if R_1 then A_1.

Whenever a valid explanation in terms of reasons is available such a conditional will be true. Such conditionals are open non-material conditionals which are true regardless of whether their antecedent is satisfied. Within the circumstances which are pre-supposed the truth of the antecedent necessitates the truth of the consequent. The claim that is being made, therefore, is that when we explain an action in terms of reasons the presence of intentional states of a kind to provide reasons for the action, (R_1), necessitates, in the circumstances, (C), the occurrence of an action of the kind explained, (A_1).

The truth of such a conditional claim requires the truth of law-like regularities, law-like in projecting to future and counterfactual cases. Acceptance of such regularities is implicit in our acceptance of the conditional. The validity of the conditional claim does not depend on its antecedent and consequent actually occurring, and we would have no ground for accepting that the consequent would follow the antecedent unless we were prepared to accept that this would be so in all similar cases.

Similar considerations apply in cases where we attribute abilities to people. Those things which an agent can do in certain circumstances are those which, if she forms appropriate intentions, she does. Her abilities are captured by a set of conditionals: if I_1 then A_1, if I_2 then A_2, etc. Here the substitutions for I_1, I_2 are the formation of certain kinds of intentions. Such conditionals can be true only if there are true generalisations linking intentions and actions of certain kinds. When an agent acts intentionally, then, what kind of action is performed is conditionally dependent on what kinds of intentional states are present.

These claims need some qualification. It may be that, when I explain my successfully potting a blue ball in snooker by my desire to score certain points, in those very circumstances I might have had the same desires, beliefs and intentions and flunked the shot. If this is possible the link between our reasons and actions may on such occasions be only probabilistic and fall short of strict necessitation. The form of the conditional supported in such cases would be:

(1*) Given C, if R_1, then probably A_1.

and the corresponding lawlike generalisation would also have a probabilistic form. More precisely, then, whenever we have a genuine reason-giving explanation, the fact that the agent has intentional states of the kind which provide her with reasons for acting, necessitates or renders probable, in those circumstances, the occurrence of an action of the kind explained.

It is not only conditionals such as (1) and (1*) which are supported by reason-giving explanations. In the envisaged example, if I do not believe the left fork leads to Dubrovnik I do not take the left fork. That is, conditionals of the form of (2) are also implied by such explanations.

(2) Given C, if not R_1, not A_1.

Reasons not only necessitate the actions they explain. In the circumstances they are also necessary for them. Again the acceptance of such a conditional claim requires the acceptance of law-like regularities; for if we are to conclude what would be the case in some non-actual situation, we can only do so on the basis of what would occur in all situations of a certain kind.

Some qualification is also needed here, for there are situations in which our actions are doubly and independently rationally justified. I may be driving along a certain street both to reach the shops and en route to pick up the children from school. Had either reason been absent I would have driven along the road anyway in pursuit of the alternative goal. In such cases (2) does not hold of either set of reasons on their own (though it holds of their disjunction). Apart from such cases, however, reason-providing intentional states form necessary conditions for the actions they explain.

The conditional dependencies of our intentional acts on our reason-providing intentional states is a key feature of reason-giving explanation, and one which any account of its explanatory force must accommodate.

2. Causal explanations and conditionals

It will be the contention of this chapter that the conditional implications just outlined in section 1 suggest that intentional explanations are causal explanations, and their supporting generalisations empirical causal laws. This argument has two components. First, it is claimed that causal explanations support conditionals of just the kind outlined. This claim is made immediately below. Secondly, no other account of intentional explanation currently on offer provides an account of the conditionals. This issue is addressed in section 4.

In cases of causal explanations there are conditional implications which exactly parallel those discussed in the previous section. For example, if a fire (at s_1 t_1) is causally explained by a match being dropped (at s_1 t_0), then in these circumstances:

(1) If a match is dropped (at $s_1 t_0$), there is a fire (at $s_1 t_1$).

(2) If a match is not dropped (at $s_1 t_0$), there is not a fire (at $s_1 t_1$).

That is, where we have causally explanatory links the causal explanans forms a necessary part of a set of conditions which are sufficient for the effect to be explained.[1] Such links of necessity and necessitation need qualification, in ways that parallel the intentional case, to allow for the possibility of probabilistic rather than deterministic causality, and for the possibility of duplicate independent explanations. Should probabilistic causal links form an objective feature of the world, rather than simply reflect our current ignorance of further relevant factors, causal explanations may point to factors which, given their accompanying circumstances, bestow a certain probability on their effect, rather than necessitate it. In cases of over-determination or preemptive causality[2] a causal explanation may invoke factors which are not necessary in these circumstances for an effect of a specified kind to occur, though they must form a necessary component of one of the sets of factors which necessitate or bestow objective probability on the effect.

The conditional implications of causal explanations require that causal sequences fall under general laws, for reasons articulated in the previous section. If we can

[1] The formulation here reflects the work of John Mackie. See Mackie 1973.

[2] Over-determination occurs when two independent sets of causal conditions are present each of which would provide a complete explanation of the effect. (Two bullets enter the heart together.) Pre-emptive causality occurs when, if one set of conditions were absent, a further and distinct set would be completed (if a man in the desert is carrying poison water which leaks out of his can).

2. Reason-giving Explanations as Causal Explanations

conclude from an antecedent of a certain kind that a consequence will follow, without either being actual, we are only able to do so in virtue of the sequence being covered by a law-like regularity. Such a necessary link between conditional claims and laws might be challenged by those who suggest that the truth conditions of conditional claims can be given in terms of possible worlds. For David Lewis,[1] for example, the appropriateness of certain conditionals is fixed by judgments of similarity across possible worlds. In a case where a ball breaks a window, the conditional claim that, if the ball does not hit it, the window remains unbroken, would be appropriate, if those possible worlds in which the ball fails to hit the window, and the window remained unbroken, are *more similar* to an actual world than those in which the window is not hit but none the less breaks. What is unclear, however, is how these judgments of similarity are to be reached. Lewis accepts that we frequently rely on general laws in reaching them, for worlds which operate on the same laws as ours are, he claims, on the whole closer to our world than those which do not. But such a guideline is not absolute. We may accept a small miracle to retain a large degree of similarity in other areas. However, if any miracles are allowed, our judgments of similarity will not obviously coincide with the conditional claims which we would accept. If we allow a small miracle, and the window breaks, although not hit, we have a world which still contains my mother's anger, the children's delight and the whole host of events which follow therefrom, and we therefore seem to have a world more similar to the actual one than the world without the miracle. Yet we would all agree that, without the ball hitting it, the window would

[1] Lewis 1973.

47

remain unbroken. It therefore seems that we cannot rely on judgments of intuitive similarity to settle the question as to which conditionals are the appropriate ones.

To accept that causal explanations, if true, require the truth of general laws is not to assume that we can spell out such laws whenever we make causal claims. Although we may often be justified in making causal claims we would usually find it difficult to characterise the total set of factors in the light of which a given occurrence necessitated, or rendered probable, its effect. This is unsurprising when we consider that causal explanations often take place against a background of normal conditions, the necessary components of which we are frequently unaware of until they are removed. Moreover necessitating or probabilising links require the absence of *defeating conditions*. The lighted match would not have caused a fire if water had been thrown over it. In given cases it might be possible for us to judge that defeating conditions are absent without it being possible to list all the defeating conditions there might be.

To adopt a covering-law model of causation does not imply that causal relations can be wholly accommodated within a pure regularity theory. At the very least causal generalisations need to be distinguished from conceptual or constitutive ones (see section 4 below). For some philosophers they require the support of some form of causal mechanism. They presuppose a certain kind of independence of cause and effect. In arguing that intentional explanations are a sub-species of causal explanation it will therefore be necessary to show not only that there can be laws linking intentional states and actions, but that these laws conform to whatever further constraints we place on the causal relation. Before proceeding to that, however, we need to look at an account, that of Donald Davidson, which while accepting causal links between intentional states and action denies the need for intentional causal laws at all.

3. Davidson's minimal causal account

Donald Davidson[1] has provided an account of reason-giving explanation which accepts: (a) that reason-giving intentional states cause action; (b) that causal claims require the support of general laws; but which rejects (c) that the generalisations linking intentional states and intentional acts have the status of causal laws.

It is therefore important to look at Davidson's account, and consider whether it can accommodate the conditionals outlined in section 1. In doing so the implications of the claim that reason-giving intentional states causally explain actions will become clearer.

For Davidson the intentional states which the agent has which provide the reasons for acting *cause*, but do not *causally explain*, her action. His account therefore rests on drawing a distinction between two distinct kinds of causal connectives:[2]

(1) 'causes': this expresses an extensional relation which holds regardless of how the events are described. So both: (i) Jack's falling down caused Jack to break his crown, and (ii) the fact that Jack fell down caused it to be the case that Jack broke his crown, are to be analysed as: 'there are events e_1 and e_2 such that e_1 is a falling down of Jack, e_2 is a breaking of his crown by Jack, and e_1 caused e_2.' Within such causal statements a relation is asserted between particular events, which will hold no matter how we describe these events. Such causal links require that there be some description of e_1 and e_2 in virtue of

[1] Davidson, 'Mental events', in Davidson 1980.
[2] Davidson, 'Causal relations', ibid.

which the sequence can be seen to be an instance of a general law, i.e. e_1 causes e_2 only if: e_1 is an X-type event, e_2 is a Y-type event, and there is a causal law linking X-type events and Y-type events as such. Singular causal statements stating the causal link between e_1 and e_2 need not, however, describe them as X events and Y events. In terms of our example there need be no general law linking fallings of Jack to crown breakings of Jack for (i) and (ii) to be true.

(2) 'causally explains': causal explanatory statements reflect the kinds linked by the causal laws governing the sequence concerned. If it is in virtue of e_1 being X and e_2 being Y that the causal link between them holds, i.e. the general law governing the case links X-type events and Y-type events, the fact that there was an X-type event causally explains the fact that there was a Y-type event. What is therefore causally explained is the occurrence of certain kinds of states of affairs or events, and this by reference to the fact that certain kinds of antecedents preceded them.

Armed with this distinction between different kinds of causal statement Davidson applies it to reason-giving explanations. He claims: (i) The intentional states which provide the reasons for which an agent performed an action *cause* (in sense (1)) that action. (ii) The causal laws which support this causal link rest, not on the intentional description of those states, but on their physical descriptions. These laws are couched not in intentional or any other psychological vocabulary, but in physical vocabulary. (iii) The intentional states which provide reasons for an action do not *causally explain* (in sense 2) that action.

The view that reason-giving explanations cause but do not causally explain actions will be termed the minimal causal account.

2. Reason-giving Explanations as Causal Explanations

Objections to the minimal causal account

Some objections to the Davidsonian account derive from his individuating conditions for events and states.[1] These objections will not be pursued here. Rather, it will be argued that, even if we accept the Davidsonian distinction, reason-giving explanations will fall into the category of causal explanations and therefore require general laws employing psychological/intentional vocabulary.

If reason-giving explanations were only statements of extensional causal relations they should sustain substitutions of the appropriate kind, that is redescriptions of the intentional states and actions concerned, without losing their explanatory power. But this is not the case. The explanatory force of intentional explanations rests on the fact that the intentional states referred to are of a kind to rationalise an action of the kind to be explained. Even if we managed to refer to particular intentional states in some other way (maybe an agent desiring a drink could be referred to as her being in a state brought about by a marathon run), we cannot necessarily substitute these alternative descriptions within reason-giving explanations. What this makes clear is that a

[1] Davidson's thesis requires an ontology of token states as particulars each one of which may be described by means of many non-synonymous sentences. This requires an account of the identity conditions of such particulars which it is difficult to provide. Davidson's own suggestion is that token events/states are identical if they share all their extensional causal relations. But this simply seems to emphasise, within his view, the interdependence of 'extensional causality' and 'token events'. Moreover 'if we analyse "a caused b" as meaning that a and b may be described in such a way that the existence of each could demonstrated, in the light of the causal laws, to be a necessary and sufficient condition of the existence of the other', then, if there are no restrictions on the descriptions of the state which we can produce, we can show there are causal

claim that intentional states are identical with physical states, linked via physical laws to behaviour, is not sufficient to accommodate the explanatory force of reference to those states *under their intentional descriptions*. Exponents of a minimal causal account therefore need to supplement it in a way that accommodates the further explanatory force of reason-giving explanations. The way in which they tend to do this is to rest the explanatory role of intentional explanations on the rationalising link between reason and action. This is thought to convey its own form of intelligibility, by showing the action to be justified or appropriate given the agent's intentional states (see Chapter One).

It is a point against the Davidsonian picture that in providing reasons for action we are doing two things, pointing to a causal link and to a rationalising one, when the two are quite independent.[1] In Chapter One we considered the suggestion that reasons explain actions simply by rationalising them, and rejected it. One basis for such rejection would not apply to the minimal causal account. It can distinguish real reasons from 'mere rationalisations' by the requirement that there be a causal link between the reason-giving intentional states and the actions. Consider, however, the case of the hypnotist. In this case there were two beliefs linked both by extensional causal relations and by reason-giving links, but it was quite inappropriate to point to the reason-giving relation between the two beliefs in

---

connections between causally unconnected states. See Davidson 1980, 157/8.

[1] Indeed at first sight it seems miraculous that intentional states should in fact regularly cause behaviour of a kind which they rationalise. Within the total Davidsonian picture, however, an assignment of intentional descriptions to token states must be presumed to take account of the behaviour which they produce.

explanations of the second, for the agent would have come to hold the second belief anyway whether or not the first had been linked to it in a reason-giving way. In such cases we regard explanation in terms of reasons as invalid, but this a Davidsonian does not appear able to accommodate.

The problem the minimal causal account faces with the hypnotist example is a consequence of its inability to explain the key conditionals which reason-giving explanations support. In pointing out this inadequacy, we need to pay attention to the exact form in which such conditionals are couched. In the case in which we explain an agent reaching out for a glass of water, the Davidsonian account can accommodate the following conditionals: (1') in the circumstances, if the agent's desire for a drink and belief that water will satisfy it are present, her reaching out to the glass of water occurs; (2') in the circumstances, if the agent's desire and belief are not present then her reaching out does not occur. In the expression of such claims 'the agent's desire', 'the agent's belief' and 'the reaching out' all refer extensionally. Their role within the conditionals is simply to pick out token events/states. Any description which picked out those states could be substituted within the conditionals *salva veritate*. The situations we are asked to envisage are those in which certain token occurrences are, or are not, present. The necessity and sufficiency in the circumstances which such conditionals point to is that of certain token states, which happen to have intentional descriptions. If those token states have physical descriptions, the physical laws governing the case can support such conditionals. For if the token occurrences are the only tokens present of the physical kinds required to bring about the effect, and sufficient for it, their presence or absence will determine whether or not the effect occurs.

However, reason-giving explanations do not only support conditionals of this extensionalist kind, but also: (1) In the circumstances if the agent has a desire for a drink and a belief that water would satisfy it, she performs an action which is a reaching for a glass of water. (2) In the circumstances, if the agent does not have a desire for a drink and a belief that water will satisfy it, she does not perform an action of reaching for a glass of water. The key point is that the conditionals invoked here are concerned with the fact that certain kinds of states are present or absent. Where reason-giving explanations are appropriate it is the fact that the agent has intentional states of certain kinds (states which rationalise the performance of a certain kind of action) which is, in the circumstances, necessary and sufficient for a certain kind of act (an act of the kind rationalised). It was just such links which were absent in the case of the hypnotist, and this was why reason-giving explanation was inapplicable there. For it was not a necessary condition of the agent coming to hold a belief of the kind she did, that her previous belief should have been of a kind to rationalise it.

Such conditional links cannot be accommodated within a minimal causal account. For within that account it is the fact that the agent's states are of certain physical kinds which is causally relevant to her behaviour. Such conditional links can be accommodated within an account which regards the agent's reason-providing intentional states as causally explanatory: i.e. one which regards the presence of states of a kind to rationalise a course of action as causally relevant to the production of behaviour of the kind rationalised. But such a view requires the support of causal generalisations linking intentional states as such, with intentional actions as such, and this is just what

54

2. Reason-giving Explanations as Causal Explanations

Davidson denies.[1]

4. Non-causal conditional links

Thus far in this chapter I have suggested that intentional explanations support certain key conditionals, and that this fact supports their interpretation as causal explanations, backed by intentional causal laws. Theorists who wish to reject this conclusion must look elsewhere for a way of accommodating such conditionals, and their corresponding generalisations. Jaegwon Kim[2] has pointed out a range of cases in which there are conditional dependencies between states of affairs but no causal links. Kim expresses his examples in counterfactual terms, but in each case open non-material conditionals expressing necessity and necessitation can be constructed, together with their corresponding generalisations. Kim's cases fall into two main types. First, there are examples of some sort of logical or conceptual dependency: 'If yesterday had not been Monday, today would not be Tuesday', 'If my sister had not given birth at t, I would not have become an uncle at t'. Secondly, there are a range of cases which reflect what might be called ontological dependency: 'If I had not turned the knob, I would not have opened the window', 'If this pot had a different molecular structure it would not be so fragile'. The relation manifested in the second range of examples has been termed *supervenience*, and will receive more extended treatment in later chapters. In cases of both logical dependency and supervenience relations of necessity and necessitation exist between

[1] For some parallel objections to the Davidsonian thesis see Honderich 'The argument for anomalism monism', *Analysis* 42, and 'Psycho-physical law-like connections and their problems', *Inquiry* 24.
[2] Kim 1973.

antecedent and consequent, and these relations are reflected in corresponding generalisations. It is therefore important to consider whether the conditional links between intentional states and behaviour could reflect either of these relations.

Could the conditional links with which we are concerned result from conceptual links between intentional states and actions? This looks like a promising place to start for there are conceptual links of some kind here (for a full discussion of them see Chapter Three). Let us consider first the conditional expressing necessitation:

(1) Given C, if R_1 then A_1

What is needed, if this is to be a case of logical dependency, is that a statement of certain conditions plus a description of the agent's reason-providing intentional states should conceptually entail that the agent acts in a certain way. Should the behaviour fail to occur the intentional description must be withdrawn. However, the conceptual links between intentional states and action are not such that the occurrence of one kind of action can be a necessary or a sufficient condition of the agent's being in a certain intentional state. The conceptual links between intentional states and action contain *ceteris paribus* clauses which are ineliminable at the conceptual level. Moreover none of our intentional states are single-track dispositions and no one kind of action in specified circumstances is necessary or sufficient to establish their presence (see Chapter Three). It is therefore not possible to accommodate:

(1) Given C, if R_1 then A_1
or
(2) Given C, if not R_1, then not A_1

by means of conceptual links alone.

2. Reason-giving Explanations as Causal Explanations

It might be suggested that, if (1) was interpreted as expressing relations of probability, it could be accommodated conceptually. Something of this suggestion is found in Davidson's 'Hempel on Explaining Action', where he argues that to attribute a desire for G to an agent at all implies that 'if the agent believes φing is a means to G, there is some (low) probability that the agent will φ'.[1] There are two problems with this. First, in cases of genuine reason giving explanation the probability attaching to the agent's action, in the light of her intentional states, is much higher than could be sustained by any such conceptual link. Secondly, it is simply not the case that even such low probabilistic links hold whenever an agent has such a desire. Whether or not there is any objective probability of the agent's so acting, in given circumstances, depends on what other desires the agent has, the state of her nervous system, etc. If these circumstances rule out her φing (maybe the appropriate nerves are cut) there is no probability that she will.

What of conditional (2), asserting the necessity of our intentional states for our intentional acts? A Davidsonian might suggest the following support for such a conditional. If the causal generalisations governing the causal link between intentional states and actions operate at the physical level, what will be causally explained in each case will be physical movements of the agent's body. In order to provide an explanation of the agent's intentional action, we need to supplement this explanation with a description of the circumstances in virtue of which these bodily movements can be redescribed as intentional actions. Part of such circumstances might well be the fact that the physical states

[1] Davidson, 1980.

causing such movements are certain kinds of intentional states. The problem with this answer is that it would, for example, render an agent having a desire for a drink necessary only for her reaching for a glass of water, where this implies intentionality. It does not make it necessary her hand moving in certain ways. It doesn't however seem plausible to claim that whenever we act intentionally the bodily movements by which we perform our intentional acts would occur anyway, whether or not they are preceded by intentional states of the appropriate kinds. That is, not only does (2) hold, but also:

(3) Given C, if not R_1, then not B-type bodily movements.

Such a conditional cannot find support in purely conceptual considerations.

If the conditional links between intentional states and behaviour cannot be accommodated via logical dependency between the two, can they be explained as reflecting a supervenience relation between them? Can we regard our intentional descriptions as depending for their truth on our behaviour in a way that would generate the required conditional links? What would be suggested here is not logical behaviourism, but ontological behaviourism. The intentional descriptions which provide our reasons for acting would be made true by the behaviour they rationalise in such a way that that behaviour provided in the circumstances a necessary and sufficient condition for the truth of the intentional descriptions. Given that behaviour, in those circumstances, we should be unable to withhold those intentional descriptions. For many Davidsonian theorists intentional descriptions do supervene on descriptions of behaviour, so this must look like the most promising way to accommodate the counterfactual and conditional claims. But this approach, of course, runs into difficulties parallel to those facing logical behaviourism. There are *no* necessary and sufficient behavioural conditions for intentional states, of a logical *or* ontological kind. Given any actual behaviour, an assignment of intentional states to a system would remain indeterminate; and this even if we are allowed to take into account a whole pattern of such behaviour (circumstances not obviously included in C). No item of behaviour is sufficient in this way for specified intentional descriptions. Neither is it necessary. Intentional descriptions can be true in the absence of any overt behaviour. Davidson recognises this, and within his overall system our intentional characterisations have the feature of indeterminacy. No behavioural conditions are sufficient for their truth, and there are no further conditions which have a bearing on it. Such a picture does not yield the conditionals we have been at pains to accommodate in this chapter. Moreover it has the added disadvantage of requiring that our intentional descriptions lack determinate truth-value. Both of these consequences give us reason to challenge the restriction of the supervenient base of our intentional states to the agent's behaviour; and to look elsewhere for an explanation of our conditional claims.

It seems therefore that it is possible to appeal neither to logical nor to ontological dependency between intentional states and behaviour to explain the conditional dependencies they display. The argument therefore remains that a causal explanatory link is the best way to explain such dependencies.[1]

---

[1] In Chapters Five and Six it will be argued that a relation of ontological dependency between intentional states and the physical antecedents of bodily movements can generate the required conditional dependencies, but in a way that supports causal explanations at the intentional level rather than dispensing with them.

CHAPTER THREE

Intentional Theory and Conceptual Connections

1. Intentional theory

What distinguishes intentional acts from mere bodily movements is their susceptibility to a certain kind of explanation – explanation in terms of the agent's intentional states. The last two chapters have investigated two features of such explanations. An action is explained by displaying its *rationality*: that is, the reason-giving links which it has to the agent's intentional states, in virtue of the intentional content of such states. The display of the rationality of the act is, however, only explanatory if the action is *causally explained* by the presence of the intentional states which make it rational to perform it.

We explain behaviour in that special way which is our concern by the successful application to the systems concerned of intentional theory. Such a theory provides for the attribution to agents of states with intentional content, and lays out the inter-connections of such states to each other, to the agents' environment and to their behaviour. It is by our grasp of such a theory that we come to understand what is required for a system to have intentional states at all, for such states are individuated by their role within explanatory intentional theory. Intentional theory has two components:

(a) It articulates the kinds of inter-connection between intentional states themselves, intentional states and actions, and intentional states and the environment, which are constitutive of rationality. In relation to the environment our intentional theory indicates what kind of intentional states are appropriate in what environmental conditions. It is only possible to do this holistically, for what environmental conditions are, for example, evidence for a belief, depends on what further intentional states the agent has. (Though for some class of beliefs, maybe perceptual beliefs, certain environmental conditions will have the status of canonical[1] evidence for them, i.e. it is *prima facie* appropriate to hold those beliefs in those conditions.) Internally our theory indicates what intentional states it is rational to hold with what others. Such reason-giving links between intentional states were characterised in Chapter One via a discussion of theoretical and practical reasoning. An action is minimally rational if it conforms to the agent's intention and rational to a higher degree if that intention was rationally formed. That there are such rationalising links between intentional states, environment and behaviour is constitutive of those states being the states they are. The pattern of rationalising links is distinct for each kind of state. Part of what we saw in Chapter One was the distinct patterns for desire, belief and intention.

(b) A causal explanatory theorist argues that our intentional theory has a second component: namely, it articulates explanatory causal links between intentional states, between intentional states and the environment, and between intentional states and action. Our theory

---

[1] Cf. Peacocke 1983, 116.

therefore contains generalisations linking such components which have the status of causal explanatory laws.

The connection between the two components of intentional theory is a complex one. It was argued in Chapter Two, contra Davidson, that the two components are not quite separate. Rather the explanatory laws linking intentional states with each other/environment/action must make essential reference to the intentional kinds of these states, including their intentional contents, and utilise the rationalising links which the first component of our intentional theory articulates. The matter is not simple, however. It is not the case that intentional states always causally produce further states/actions which they jointly rationalise or are always produced by appropriate environmental conditions. This is the case even when the reason-giving links are as strong as they could be. Even if a belief deductively supports another, the second belief may not be held; and we may act contrary to what we believe the best action to be. The fact that certain rationalising links hold between states is therefore not sufficient alone to ensure that causal links will also hold between such states, at least for agents who are less than perfectly rational. To produce a set of causally sufficient conditions for an intentional act, we need to add to the fact that the agent has intentional states which rationalise such an act, some further conditions to guarantee that an act of the appropriate kind is performed. What is clear, however, is this: in cases of intentional explanation a causally necessary factor in the production of the action is the existence of rationalising links between constituents of the explanans and explanandum.

If a system can be attributed intentional states at all, there will be some circumstances[1] in which these states

[1] It might be thought that the claim that there be some circumstances C in which given intentional states lead to action is

will produce further states/actions of a kind which they rationalise, where such consequents would not be produced by these further circumstances alone, and where the kind of states/actions which are produced depends on which are rationalised by the agent's intentional states. This is the condition which we grasp in grasping what is required for a system to have intentional states. At the present stage of knowledge what these further conditions are for each such causal inter-action is not fully known. This has the consequence that the general principles in terms of which an intentional theory is articulated have the character not of fully complete laws but of what Grice[1] calls 'law-allusiveness'. They serve rather to claim that there are laws of certain kinds, than to express such laws. Consider the following examples:

'If an agent desires G and believes φing to be a means to G, has no over-riding desires, is able and believes she is able to φ (and perhaps recognises that these attitudes make φing the thing to do, or in Grice's terms joins these desires/beliefs), she will (probably) ψ';

'If an agent intends to φ at t, and believes that t has arrived, she will (probably) φ, if she is able'.

Reference in these principles both to the agent's 'ability to φ' and to 'over-riding desires' appears to trivialise them.

---

trivialisable. (See Peacocke 1979a, 12 for a similar point.) For, to quote Peacocke 'for *any p* and *q* at all, it is *a priori* that there is some condition C such that if *p* and C obtains, then *q*. (Just take the condition $p \supset q$ itself).' To avoid trivialisation a restriction has emerged within the theory of scientific explanation generally. 'This is roughly that it must, as things actually are, be possible to verify the singular sentences of the explanans without thereby either verifying the explanandum or falsifying the remainder of the explanans.'
[1] Grice 1975.

An over-riding desire is simply a desire which over-rides, or prevents the agent from pursuing an end which she would otherwise pursue. An agent is able to act in a certain way if her intention to so act, together with her belief that the moment for action has arrived, produces the action. The presence of such apparently trivialising conditions within the general principles should be taken as making a claim that *there is a law* linking the items referred to, a claim that there are conditions which together with the intentional states specified would yield a total set sufficient for, or bestowing objective probability on, an action of the kind specified. These further conditions, however, will clearly vary according to the contents of the desires and beliefs and intention concerned. We expect some theory which will state when one desire will over-ride another, but it will clearly be crucial what kinds of desires are involved, and moreover may vary between the different agents/systems who can be attributed the same kind of desires. Equally clearly the conditions required for an agent to be able to perform a certain act, e.g. the state of her efferent nerves, will vary according to what kind of act is under consideration. Consideration of ability conditions alone, however, makes it clear that such laws include elements which do not have a psychological characterisation. The perform-ance of basic actions requires moving our bodies in ways dependent on our efferent nerves functioning properly. Any law linking intentions with such actions must therefore include among its antecedents the fact that they do so. The laws governing intentional agents will therefore include both intentional and physiological vocabulary. The point is reinforced when we consider the causal link not only of intentional states and actions, but, what is equally important, the causal link of intentional states and states of the agent's environment. For a state to count as a belief it must be sensitive to evidence: that is, to states of affairs which have a bearing on its truth or falsity. The set of conditions, including crucially for perceptual beliefs the state of our sensory apparatus, required to yield such sensitivity in our beliefs is not something which we can at present fully specify. But we do know that for an agent to have beliefs some conditions ensuring such sensitivity must be present. This is not to require that our beliefs be foolproof, but that the mechanisms of belief production must allow, overall, such sensitivity.

There is a further constraint which our intentional theory sets on the nature of its explanatory laws which needs to be mentioned. This concerns a particular kind of sensitivity which is required between our intentional states and their causes and effects, which serves to emphasise the importance of rationalising links to such causal explanations. Consider the following example. A waitress wishes to embarrass her employer. She works out that a way to do this would be to drop a pile of glasses in front of some guests. She may even form the intention to drop the glasses. At this point however her audacity at forming such an intention so unnerves her that she drops the glasses! Here we would be unhappy to claim that her behaviour could be explained as an intentional act for which she had reasons, despite the fact that reason-giving intentional states provided a part of the causal explanation of how she came to act as she did. In an important sense it seems fortuitous, a happy accident, that the agent's nervousness produced behaviour which was just the kind that she had reason to perform. In cases of genuine reason-giving explanations we require that the link between intentional states and action should not be of this fortuitous kind. Christopher Peacocke in *Holistic*

Explanation[1] gives this issue extended treatment and puts forward a condition for genuine intentional explanation: namely, that the intentional states invoked in such explanation should *differentially explain* the agent's intentional acts. Such a requirement is also taken to hold between the features of the agent's environment, and the intentional states which they produce. It is probably simplest to capture this notion by means of an example. If I am using a 'test your strength' machine, how high the needle goes up the dial is differentially explained by how hard I pull on the handle. In Peacocke's terms there is a function linking how hard I push with the degree to which the needle moves. This notion cannot be captured purely in terms of necessary and sufficient conditions. My pulling is necessary for the movement of the needle, but so are lots of other conditions which do not bear the same functional relation to the degree which the needle moves. Peacocke claims that the kind of functional dependency invoked here should be a feature of the intentional laws governing our intentional actions. Crudely, conditions must be such that what kind of action is produced is a function of what intentional states with which contents precede it, and, of course, the differential explanation requirement will also govern the causal inter-relations between intentional states, and their causal origins in the world. The condition of differential explanation is one which requires much greater attention and refinement than can be given to it here. Further references will be found in the footnotes.[2] I

---

[1] Peacocke 1979a, ch. 2.

[2] For detailed discussion of what has been called the problem of deviant causal chains, apart from Peacocke, see Davidson, 'Freedom to act', in Davidson 1980, Pears 1975, Morton 1975, Davies 1983. For a refinement of the notion of functional dependency in terms of a route which gives the possibility of an agent's knowledge of what she is about to do, see Charles 1984a, 92-107.

will however adopt it as a constraint on the laws constituting our intentional theory that they ensure that the
rationalising links are differentially explanatory.

Our intentional theory, then, is not complete, nor
closed. Nor should we expect it to be. It does, however,
have a core structure of the form outlined here, specifying
the rationalising and interdependent causal networks
within which our intentional states are located and which
provides them with their individuating conditions A
grasp of this core, including its law-allusive principles,
seems essential if we are to understand what it is for a
system to have intentional states and act intentionally.

Given that the individuation of our intentional kinds
derives from their location in our explanatory intentional
theory, the core principles of such theory have an *a priori*
status. Such a feature has been thought to threaten the
claim of such a theory to be causally explanatory. One
often quoted argument sees conceptual connections
between intentional states and behaviour which undermine the possibility of empirical causal ones. This argument will be addressed in section 4 below. For some
theorists the *a priori* elements of intentional theory reveal
the stipulative nature of our intentional kinds. They
cannot therefore be regarded as 'cutting nature at its
joints' in the way required for causal explanation. Consideration of this objection is addressed in section 3. Here
it is worth observing that the core principles of intentional
theory do not provide a full articulation of it. They rather
provide a characterisation of the theoretical and explanatory purposes which our taxonomy into intentional
kinds is designed to serve. A filling in of this framework by
empirical means does not therefore hold the threat of a
change of subject, so long as such explanatory structures
remain in place.

2. Can intentional laws be completed?

One objection which might be raised to the picture
outlined is the claim that the law-allusive generalisations which presently govern our intentional explanations, and serve to define our intentional kinds, cannot
in principle be completed. They cannot be supplemented
in a way that would yield causal explanatory laws. What
might motivate such a position? One thought might be
this. The principles governing our intentional attributions contain *ceteris paribus* clauses, and it might not
be possible to specify by means of a list all the factors the
presence of which might prevent the satisfaction of the
consequents of such principles, given the satisfaction of
their antecedents. If I believe p and recognise that p
implies q, *ceteris paribus*, if I continue to believe p, I
believe q. But I might none the less withhold belief, and
in considering the factors which might lead me to do this
we might have no way of knowing that a list is
exhaustive. The presence of such *ceteris paribus* clauses
does not however prevent generalisations from law-like
status (cf. Chapter Two), for such clauses are also found
among the laws of physics. Outside the domain of closed
systems many physical laws require such clauses.
Consider the Law of Gravitation, namely that 'two bodies
exert a force between each other which varies inversely
as the square of the distance between them and varies
directly as the product of their masses'.[1] Such a law as it
stands does not hold. If for example the bodies are
charged, the force between them does not accord with
this law. It may well be that we could not produce a list of
all the factors which would modify the forces in this way.
The presence of a *ceteris paribus* clause in such laws need

[1] Richard Feynman, *The Character of Physical Law*, Cambridge,
Mass. 1967, 14 quoted by Cartwright 1983, 57.

not effect their explanatory use on any occasion, as long as it is determinately true, regarding any application of the law, whether there were any such modifying factors present. The same can be true in the intentional case. (A distinct point, made in Chapter Two, but worth reiterating here, is that genuine laws can also be of a probabilistic nature.)

The worry about turning our law-allusive principles into genuine laws may however have a different source. Very different kinds of systems may possess states which conform to our core principles, but the mechanisms by which they do so may be different in different cases. A bat may have states sensitive to environmental conditions and guide its behaviour in a way that accommodates them, but it has very different sensory apparatus from ours. It therefore does not seem possible to complete a general law linking environmental conditions to, for example, perceptual beliefs, in a way that would apply to all intentional systems. This however is not really a problem. The kind of generality required to render our intentional explanations causally explanatory is that, on each occasion that such an explanation is proffered, conditions be such that it is generally true that in such conditions a consequent of that kind would follow (or probably follow) from an antecedent of that kind. The particular law which governs the explanation in the case of the bat will be distinct from that governing our perceptual interactions, though each will be general in form, applying to all creatures with particular kinds of sensory apparatus. The possibility that the laws governing different kinds of entities which are intentional might be distinct, even the possibility that different human beings may satisfy different laws (consider what happens when we substitute prosthetic devices), should not be a cause for concern. To qualify for intentionality

69

all that is required is that all such laws should conform to the law-allusive principles at the core of our intentional theory. The distinct particular laws will simply reflect the range of different conditions by means of which the required sensitivity between environment, intentional states and behaviour can be achieved.

3. Intentional kinds as natural kinds?

There is an argument, put forward in the work of Colin McGinn[1] that intentional kinds cannot be regarded as natural kinds and therefore cannot feature in genuine causal explanations. The objection derives from the *a priori* elements within intentional theory. McGinn's argument starts from an account of the semantic features of natural kind terms originating in the work of Kripke and Putnam,[2] and developed by many others, for example Richard Boyd.[3] Central to such an account is a *realism* about natural kinds. Our aim in constructing such kinds is to 'cut nature at its joints'.[4] Classification into such kinds is intended to group together entities in a way that reflects (real) causal features of the world. For McGinn a consequence of such realism is that terms for such kinds are regarded as having *a posteriori*, *natural* definitions, rather than *a priori*, *stipulative* ones. Our original naive divisions may require revision as science advances and the features which prompt them are regarded, not as providing necessary and sufficient conditions for membership of the kind, but rather as attempts to fix the reference of a kind whose essential

[1] McGinn 1978.
[2] Kripke 1980. H. Putnam, 'Explanation and reference' and 'The meaning of meaning', in Putnam 1975.
[3] Boyd 1979, 1982, 1984a.
[4] Cf. Plato *Phaedrus* 265E (quoted by Boyd 1984a).

properties it will be the task of scientific investigation to uncover. With the advance of science we discover, for example, that some things which we took to be gold are not really gold, but only fool's gold. In McGinn's terms 'scientific realism' requires 'that our commonsense intellectual organisation of a given subject-matter might be substantially modified by, and be defeasible in the face of, a projected scientific theory'.[1]

McGinn argues that it is not possible to adopt such an attitude to our mental terms. Their definitions are not natural and *a posteriori*, he claims, but stipulative and *a priori*. It is not possible to regard the characteristics by means of which we currently individuate intentional kinds, which include their role in explaining action, as mere reference fixing devices. Such roles are essential to states being of those kinds, and mastery of our intentional concepts requires grasp of that role. Our judgments concerning the conditions under which creatures satisfy the same intentional predicates appear to embody no assumptions that such creatures must share other common characteristics, e.g. physical ones, or other yet to be discovered psychological ones. Should a system satisfy the 'laws and quasi-laws' of our intentional theory, we would not refuse to attribute intentionality to it on discovery that such further states differed from ours. Such considerations make it difficult to regard our intentional terms as names for yet to be discovered essences, and their *a priori* links to action as simply a consequence of our reference-fixing practices. (These considerations link to the anti-reductionist arguments discussed in the following chapter.) McGinn concludes from this that intentional terms have stipulative rather than natural definitions and cannot be regarded as natural kinds.

[1] McGinn 1978.

McGinn's conclusions, however, are too swift. First, even if our current intentional theory contains necessary and sufficient conditions for the attribution of intentional states, this in itself does not rule out the possibility of our discovering other conditions to be also necessary. Moreover from the fact that our present law-allusive intentional generalisations contain *a priori* elements, as a consequence of the implicit definition of our intentional kinds within them, we do not have to conclude that they are purely stipulative. McGinn compares such terms to artefact terms such as clocks and chairs, but such a comparison is misleading. Such terms are purely stipulative, and our purposes in classifying by means of them is purely descriptive. The matter is quite otherwise with our intentional schema. Its purpose is explanatory. It is designed to capture causal regularities in the world. To quote Richard Boyd:

> The naturalness of natural kinds (properties etc.) lies in the way in which they reflect features of the causal structure of the world which are important in theoretical understanding, explanation and inductive generalisation.[1]

Our system of classification into intentional kinds serves just such a purpose. It explains our behavioural interaction with our environment. Moreover the generalisations which constitute our intentional theory have been tested from time immemorial, and govern all of our everyday interactions with intentional agents. Merely stipulative definitions of kinds, e.g. artefacts, do not lead to the generation of complex bodies of law-like generalisations. What more can we require of classifications which reflect the real structure of reality, than

[1] Boyd 1984a.

that they allow the formulation of a body of explanatory theory which is instantiated by parts of the world? It would seem that the key test of the naturalness of our kind terms, within the realist construal, should not be whether their definitions are *a priori* or *a posteriori*, but whether the system of classification which they reflect allows the formulation of law-like generalisations which the world, as thus classified, satisfies. In this sense of natural kind our intentional terms appear to qualify.

4. The logical connection argument

It is frequently claimed that where we have instances of causal explanation the link between explanans and explanandum must be empirical and *a posteriori*. This condition goes back to Hume, and his insistence that cause and effect must be *distinct existences*. There is a tradition which regards intentional explanation as failing this requirement, as the connection between explanans and explanandum is *a priori*, or in some sense logical. Some forms in which this argument have been put seem quite misguided. The rationalising links between intentional states, and intentional states and intentional acts, outlined in Chapter One, are in some sense logical links between the contents of our intentional states, but they in no way entail that the states which have such contents fail the test of distinct existence. Even where one belief deductively entails another I might hold the first without the second. We might come closer to the heart of the difficulty with the claim that for genuine causal explanation it should be possible to verify the explanans independently of the explanandum. The emphasis, however, on verification may mislead us into thinking the concerns here are epistemological rather than ontological. For what is at issue is that the truth of the explanans should not require the truth of the explanandum in other than a causal way. This, of course, is a condition which seems necessary to avoid the danger of triviality or self-explanation.

When we look at the explanation of an individual intentional act it seems, at first sight, to avoid the difficulty in this form too. Even taking the most difficult case, that of intention, it seems perfectly possible that I should intend a φ-type action at t; and yet fail to produce such an action, and this even if we include the specification that ability and knowledge conditions are satisfied. The matter is more complex than this would suggest, however. What we know *a priori* is that if A intends to φ there must be some circumstances C, such that if they obtained A would (probably) φ, where circumstances C, alone, are not sufficient for the agent's φing. That is, a state is determined as being an intention to φ by the fact that it will, in some circumstances produce a φ action. However, if this is the case, it seems as if its being an intention of this kind cannot be used to explain its production of such an action, without our being involved in some kind of triviality or self-explanation. Similar points can be made concerning the intentional states of desire and belief. Neither of these states is linked simpliciter to the behaviour of the agents whose states they are. Any desire can be linked to any behaviour given the assumption of the appropriate belief, and vice versa. It is none the less true that the fact that an agent has a certain desire and belief is at least partially determined by the fact that in some circumstances the agent will produce actions which such desires and beliefs jointly rationalise, and it is just such actions which we invoke these states to explain. What threatens our intentional explanations is the triviality of virtus

74

dormitiva examples. An agent's φing is explained by reference to states whose individuating conditions require that they are liable to produce actions of this kind. Our virtus dormitiva example would not be rescued by the suggestion that to have the property of virtus dormitiva a drug must have only the tendency to produce sleep, such that it is possible to have such a property even were it to fail in sleep production on a particular occasion.

If this is a problem it is one to which a solution must be sought within the domain of intentional theory itself, if we are to maintain the claim that our intentional descriptions themselves do causal explanatory work. We cannot look to putative links between intentional states and physical states to accommodate the informativeness of the intentional level of description.[1] Even if there were some kind of token identity between mental and physical states and thereby such states shared their extensional causal properties, this would not be true of their explanatory links. Explanation is concerned with events/states in so far as they are of certain general kinds and it is not possible to substitute alternative descriptions of the same event/state within an explanation and retain its truth value (see Chapter Two). Of course if intentional terms *named physical kinds*, the properties they named would be quite independent of the actions explained. Such a possibility would, however, require reductive type identities between intentional and physical kinds which, it will be argued in Chapter Four, cannot hold. The link to the physical which does seem possible, namely a physical grounding for our intentional descriptions (see Chapter Five) will not help us here. For we are not making claims about such groundings by

[1] Contra Pettit, in McDowell & Pettit 1986, 27/8.

our intentional descriptions (as is shown by the fact that any given type of grounding may change and yet our intentional characterisation remain unchanged). We therefore have to show, from within the resources of our intentional theory, how the triviality of virtus dormitiva is avoided.

The first thing to notice is that in attributing a given set of intentional states to an agent, what we are attributing is in no way exhausted by the claim that the agent is in a state liable, in some circumstances, to produce an action of the kind to be explained. Let us look first at a minimal intentional explanation of an agent performing a φ action by means of her intention to φ. Such an intention is not just a disposition to perform such an action, given the satisfaction of ability conditions, opportunity, and the agent's belief that these conditions are satisfied. Intentions are propositional attitudes with a content which links them not only forwards to the performance of a particular kind of action, but backwards to the intentional states which provide the reasons for them. An intention is a state which causally derives from certain rationalising desires and beliefs of the agent, whose content bears relations of rationality or irrationality to the agent's total set of desires and beliefs (see Chapter One), and it involves the agent in believing that she has some chance of performing the action as a consequence of forming the intention. It is moreover a state liable to produce a different bodily movement, had the agent believed that to be an instantiation of the intentional act desired, or an action at a different time had the agent believed some other time to be the appropriate moment for that intentional act. It is these further repercussions of our intentional descriptions which are to provide the key to deflecting charges of triviality. Such repercussions are, of course, even more clearly evident when we explain an agent's actions by citing the desires and beliefs which furnish the spelt out rational justification for them. For each desire and belief is individuated by its location in a complex body of theory, linking it to a possibly infinite set of dispositions to behave in certain ways (when combined with other intentional states), to modifications in the agent's environment, and to other intentional states.

The problem is not removed, however, simply by noting that any intentional attribution has repercussions beyond a liability to produce intentional behaviour of a kind which it is invoked to explain. An example of Christopher Peacocke's makes this clear:

> Suppose a drug d both puts people to sleep and causes giddiness if taken with alcohol. Let's introduce an expression 'H(E)', any object x is H if x puts people to sleep and causes giddiness if taken with alcohol. It is not an acceptable explanation of d's putting someone to sleep that it has the property H.[1]

The reason for the unsatisfactory nature of this explanation, as it stands, is clear. The further condition of attributing H to a drug, over and above its disposition to cause sleep, need not in itself bear any relation to the sleep-putting. The co-existence of the two features of the drug may be quite accidental. In the intentional case this is not so. The cluster of properties which individuate our intentional states are a cluster that are conditionally and counterfactually interdependent.[2] The further repercussions of attributing a desire G over and above a disposition, in combination with belief B, to produce a particular action, will be properties whose presence

[1] Peacocke 1979a.
[2] Here I am indebted to Hempel 1965, 457-63.

77

provides, in the circumstances, necessary and sufficient (or probabilising) conditions for the desire as a whole, and thereby for the disposition to perform the action to be explained. For those who formulate the issue in terms of verification, the further repercussions can be used to verify the presence of the desire independently of the action to be explained. In this way the spectre of *virtus dormitiva* and the triviality of self-explanation is avoided.

At this point we can see the importance a physical base could have in grounding our intentional descriptions. Our intentional descriptions attribute complex sets of interconnected dispositions. For many people it is difficult to accept that such dispositional claims can be 'barely true', particularly when the dispositions are unactualised. Rather they require some categorical grounding to make them true. If we are materialists then we assume that such categorical grounding will be provided by the agent's physical states. The relation between intentional and physical descriptions forms the subject-matter of ensuing chapters, but at this stage an objection might immediately be raised. If the physical is needed to make true our intentional descriptions, is the physical level not the real level of explanation of action? We should not, however, conclude, from the fact that intentional descriptions make demands of our physical organisation, that the most appropriate level of explanation for action is the physical one. We have emphasised above that our intentional descriptions are not naming physical kinds. This point will be defended in the next chapter, where it is argued that the explanatory work of our intentional descriptions cannot be captured at the physical level. The physical may have ontological primacy, if we are materialists. It does not necessarily have explanatory primacy.

3. Intentional Theory and Conceptual Connections

In *Holistic Explanation*, however, Christopher Peacocke has produced a constraint on genuine causal explanation which, he claims, intentional explanations, as thus construed, would fail to meet. This constraint, termed by Peacocke 'the conjunction requirement' has its origin in the following intuition concerning genuine explanation: If some state of affairs, Fa, is explicable by reference to some law, L, together with antecedent conditions C_1 and some further state of affairs, Fb, is explicable by reference to L and some conditions C_2, then it should be possible genuinely to explain the conjunction Fa and Fb, by reference to L, C_1 and C_2. If this condition is to be satisfied without returning to the problem of self-explanation then it must not be the case that we use Fa to verify the presence of any of the conditions used to explain Fb, or use Fb to verify the presence of any of the conditions used to explain Fa. More formally the restriction is expressed as follows:

> Consider a given covering law L, and consider all the explanations which have L as their covering law ... Let $E(a)$ be the set of all singular premises that occur in some explanation that has L as its covering law; let $F(a)$ be the set of all sentences that are the explanandum sentence of some such explanation. Then the conjunction restriction requires that it is possible, as things actually are, to verify any finite conjunction of sentences in $E(a)$ without verifying any sentence in $F(a)$.[1]

Peacocke defends the intuition which generates this requirement by reference to the example of a machine, M. This machine has two display panels, and has the multi-track disposition that, 'for any natural number n, if n is displayed on its first panel, that $Q(n)$ is displayed on its second panel'. We use the term having 'a Q-property'

[1] Peacocke 1979a, 147.

for any machine having such a disposition. 'That is *all* that is meant by "has the Q-property". In particular to say that something has the Q-property is not to hypothesise an underlying mechanism responsible for the presence of the many-tracked disposition.'[1] Peacocke argues that we would not consider that we had explained any particular display on the second panel of our machine M by pointing out that the machine had a Q-property and that the display on the first panel was of a certain kind. This despite the fact that we could verify the presence of the Q-property independently of the particular display that we were explaining. What is wrong, Peacocke suggests, is that we cannot verify the presence of the Q-property independently of *all* the behaviour which reference to the property is invoked to explain. The problem expressed non-epistemically is this. In attributing to a system a two-track disposition all we are claiming is that in certain circumstances it will behave in these two ways. If we then explain its behaving in these *two ways* simply by reference to its dispositional property, the explanation seems at best trivial.

If we accept Peacocke's restrictions it might seem that intentional explanations fail to conform to them, for many of the further repercussions of our intentional descriptions, which I have argued rescues them from triviality, concern dispositions to produce further behaviour, or other intentional states. Yet such behaviour and the production of such intentional states are items which, in different circumstances, we would use the intentional state concerned to explain.

It is of course true that our intentional theory locates our intentional kinds by more than their dispositional properties. They are located also in relation to the

[1] Op. cit., 147.

environmental conditions in which they occur, to changes in which they are causally sensitive. In response to Peacocke's requirement, it might be suggested that such features of our intentional kinds could be used to individuate them, without concern for their causal output. The problems with such a suggestion emerge however even in the simplest cases of perceptual belief. Were we to attempt to establish the intentional content of such beliefs, how would we distinguish which stages of the incoming causal chain to fix on, in the absence of considering which aspects of the environment the state disposed the agent to act on discriminately? Moreover how do we decide which of an agent's states, causally and differentially sensitive to environmental conditions, to count as beliefs? What excludes states, for example, of the agent's retina, except for their dispositional properties? When we consider more complex beliefs, and the task of distinguishing beliefs/desires/intentions from each other, a consideration of their dispositions, both to produce further intentional states, and to produce behaviour, seems indispensable.

It is however possible to scrutinise the conjunction requirement, and the intuitions which support it, more carefully, in a way that undermines its challenge to intentional explanation. The intuition that was invoked concerned cases where there were actual states of affairs Fa and Fb, both explained by reference to some property. In such cases it seemed plausible to require that such a property could be invoked in explaining the conjunction of Fa and Fb. In the intentional case however both: (a) the dispositional properties of any intentional state may well be infinite; and (b) the dispositions of any state are such that they can never all be manifested conjointly.

A consequence of this is that whatever conjunction of actual explananda are offered they do not exhaust what we were attributing to a system in attributing such an intentional state to it. The presence of a given intentional state is always compatible with the absence of any set of explananda which it is invoked to explain, and is therefore sufficiently independent to play an explanatory role with regard to such a set. We should be suspicious of adopting the conjunction requirement in any stronger form than this, for if we do it will rule out as genuinely explanatory the use of any theoretical terms whose individuating conditions rest on their role within an explanatory theory. And this is to exclude too much! (Think of the explanatory use of *force*.) Peacocke himself attempts to block such a widespread exclusion as a consequence of his constraint by restricting the conjunction requirement to the relation between explanans and explananda governed by one covering law. There are problems with such a restriction. It seems *ad hoc* and unmotivated by the intuition which supported the requirement initially. It also raises problems concerning how laws are to be individuated. If it was accepted, however, the requirement would no longer be broken by intentional explanation. For it is clear that if our intentional explanations are to fall foul of the conjunction requirement thus restricted, the distinct manifestations of each of our intentional states must be explicable by reference to one covering law. But this does not appear to be the case. It is true that there are certain *a priori* principles which govern our intentional states, from which the consequences of attributing such states to a system are at least partially derived. Such general principles, however, have the characteristic already discussed of law-allusiveness. It is only by filling out such principles with specification of particular ability conditions, and the conditions under which one desire will over-ride another, that we will reach the covering laws which in fact govern the effect which occurs. These covering laws will be distinct for different kinds of effect. The implausibility of viewing the different manifestations of a particular intentional state as resting on one covering law are added to when we consider the role of such states in the production of introspective knowledge, the consistency requirements on beliefs and the causal ancestry of certain desires, together with their characteristic manifestations in feelings.

The question remains whether we should accept the conjunction requirement, even for cases to which it does apply, such as Peacocke's machine. Are we right to reject as a potential explanation of the reading on the second dial one which refers to the machine's Q-property, together with the reading on the first dial? Peacocke's presentation of this example may make it appear that we are not allowed to assume any mechanism linking the properties here. Then if we are realists about dispositions we will find the case mysterious. But his actual point was that 'Q-property' is not the *name* of some underlying property, characterised non-dispositionally. It is quite in order to assume some mechanism to be present. But if that is the case, it may look as if the real explanation would be given in terms of that mechanism. Certainly some explanation will be available in such terms, though only of certain arrangements of dots on the screens, not of their having certain readings. Under what circumstances then might we imagine that the readings might have causal explanations in their own terms, by means of the Q-property? Let us suppose a number of different instances of the Q-property, with the appropriate conditional inter-dependencies between the readings, but with distinct mechanisms in each case. Imagine also that the presence of such Q-properties forms part of a theoretical articulation of parts of the world, such that such inter-dependencies can be regarded as a feature of reality. (Maybe here we can motivate Peacocke's requirement that the property occur in more than one general law.) Then I think our claim that reference to the Q-property is non-explanatory would be undermined, for it would be required to capture a regularity not otherwise capturable.

Whatever our intuitions in the case of the machine, however, the intentional case is distinct from it in ways that allow it to escape whatever force we can allow the conjunction requirement to have.

5. Conclusion

Our intentional kinds gain their individuating conditions from within a body of intentional theory explaining an agent's mediation of her environment. Such explanations are both rationalising and causally explanatory. A world in which such explanatory structures cannot be uncovered is a world without intentional states. This implicit definition of our intentional kinds generates *a priori* links between intentional states, environment and behaviour. It has been argued that these *a priori* links are compatible with regarding the explanations which make reference to such kinds as causal ones, and thereby compatible with regarding intentional kinds as natural kinds.

Much of the rest of the book will be concerned to investigate the consequences of the view of intentional theory developed in Chapters One to Three, for the relations between the mental and the physical.

CHAPTER FOUR

Anti-reductionism and Psycho-physical Laws

1. The orthodoxy

There is an orthodoxy in recent work[1] which this chapter and the two following will try to challenge. It is this. If we regard intentional explanations as causal explanations, certain quite strong reductive connections would be required between the psychological and the physical. These reductive links do not hold. We therefore have to reject a causal explanatory view of intentional explanations. This argument is located within a framework which is both materialist and physicalist. It is materialist in assuming that psychological states are in some sense constituted out of physical states. It is physicalist, in the sense I am using this term, in assuming that all physical changes are susceptible to physical explanations. I do not wish to challenge this framework, and will return to a detailed discussion of it in the following chapter. What I want rather to defend is the coherence of a set of positions, a causal explanatory view of intentional explanation, anti-reductionism and some recognisable form of materialism and physicalism.

[1] See Davidson 1980, essays 11-13; McDowell 1985; McGinn 1978, 1980; C. & G. MacDonald 1987; G. MacDonald 1986. Papineau 1980.

After a discussion of the nature of reduction, this chapter will be primarily concerned with anti-reductionist arguments and a consideration of the extent to which they are believed to rule out intentional causal laws. I shall not be opposing the anti-reductionist claims put forward but rather disputing some of the conclusions which are drawn from them. The following chapter will then look directly at the demands made by materialism.

When we are discussing the reduction of the mental or psychological to the physical it is useful to have in mind individuating conditions for what, at least initially, appear distinct categories. It is notoriously difficult to provide such individuating conditions. In this book, however, our concern is with intentional explanation, and the focus of attention will therefore be whether theories employing intentional vocabulary can be reduced to theories using only extensional terms. Within such a characterisation the 'physical' includes terms which have extensional functional individuating conditions. Functional kinds are individuated by means of causal properties and are uncommitted regarding the intrinsic or categorical nature of the states which realise them. The attempt to reduce mental kinds to functional kinds will be directly addressed in Chapter Five.

2. What is reduction?

If it is claimed that the mental or intentional reduces to the physical, there are at least four different things whose reduction is at issue. In characterising what reduction would require in each case I shall be guided by the notion that to reduce some item to another is to show that where we may have thought there were two distinct items there turns out to be only one; and that one more accurately or perspicaciously characterised in terms of

86

the reducing vocabulary.

(a) *Predicates*: A reductive claim here would require that our intentional predicates be analysed or explicated in terms of physical predicates. This may seem an implausibly strong kind of reduction to seek, and moreover reduction of a kind not found in our favoured models (see below).

(b) *Particulars*: A reductive claim regarding particulars would require that all psychological particulars (objects or events) were identical with or constituted out of particulars individuated within physical theory. For many this forms a minimal requirement of materialism. All recognise however that an identity between, e.g., mental events and physical events, would not be sufficient to support causal explanations at the psychological level (see Chapter Two). Indeed Davidson, who argues against psychological causal explanations, none the less accepts the token identity of mental and physical events.[1] When reduction is put forward as necessary for causal explanations at the psychological level to be vindicated, more than identity of particulars is required.

(c) *Properties or kinds*: I shall run these together, taking distinctions between psychological kinds to mark distinctions between psychological properties. Most of the key arguments in this area concern the attempt to reduce mental kinds to physical kinds. In distinguishing reduction of kinds from reduction of predicates we are assuming that there are criteria for property or kind identity independent of the identity of the predicates by means of which such kinds are captured. One criterion which is agreed is that where kinds are identical they must necessarily be co-extensive (though there is some disagreement whether the necessity is merely physical or

[1] Davidson 1980, essay 11.

also metaphysical). Such necessary co-extensiveness is not sufficient for kind-identity, however. (Particularly if the necessity is only physical. We can easily think of properties, co-extensive as a consequence of physical law, but clearly distinct, e.g., creature with a heart and creature with kidneys.)) What we need to add to the condition of necessary co-extensiveness to yield conditions sufficient for property or kind reduction connects with explanation. There must be no explanatory work done by the reduced property which cannot be done by the reducing property. This requirement has several aspects. First any laws concerning the reduced property or kind must be ones which the reducing property obeys (see below). Moreover any effects which the reduced property is invoked to explain must be explicable via the reducing property.[1]

(d) *Laws*: Reduction with respect to laws requires derivation of the laws of the reduced theory from those of the reducing theory. For some writers[2] derivation of laws is all that such reduction amounts to. But this doesn't seem quite right. One law may be derivable from others simply on the basis of law-like co-extensiveness between terms which occur in each. Whether such derivation yields equivalence of the laws seems dependent on the kind of relation which such co-extensiveness reflects. What must be assured for genuine reduction is that the explanatory work of the higher-level law is captured solely by reference to the reducing level.

3. Classical models and the unity of science

When the reduction of the mental to the physical is discussed people commonly have in mind certain

[1] For parallel requirements see Putnam 1988, 77.
[2] E.g. G. MacDonald 1986.

successful reductions within the physical sciences which are taken as the model for the reductive relation between theories within different discourses. The examples referred to are the reduction of temperature to mean kinetic energy, and thereby thermo-dynamics to statistical mechanics; the reduction of water to H_2O and of lightning to electricity. As classically interpreted, in such cases we have reduction of properties or kinds and reduction of laws. Schematically:

$$S_1 \rightarrow S_2 \text{ law of reduced theory}$$

law like bi-conditionals (bridge laws)

$$P_1 \rightarrow P_2 \text{ law of reducing theory}$$

Standardly the bridge laws are regarded as identity claims. By their means the laws of the reduced theory can be derived from those of the reducing theory.

There are several important points to notice about such cases. First, the bridge laws express pairings between *unique* kinds from each level of theory. Crucially the reducing kind can be projectibly individuated from within the resources of the reducing theory and is located within a systematic body of laws there. Secondly, the effects explicable via the reduced property can be explained by the body of reducing theory. In order that this can be done such effects must be characterisable in such a way that the reducing theory can be recognised to explain them, within the resources of its own vocabulary. This indeed is one of the main ways in which the bridge laws linking the terms of each are defended. P_1's ability to explain S_2 must not simply be a consequence of the reduction. It is a necessary condition of establishing it. As a consequence of these features there is no explanatory work which is done by the reduced theory, not captured by the reducing one. Thirdly, such reduction is *asymmetric*. This is not evident from its schematic form, for the bridge laws in the classical case are *bi*-conditionals and this would appear to render the higher- and lower-level laws co-derivable. But this is reduction and the reducing theory is regarded as more fundamental, explaining the success of the one which is reduced. This explanatory power rests primarily on the greater *generality* of the lower-level laws. They fit into a body of theory of which the specified regularity ($P_1 \rightarrow P_2$) will be only one manifestation, in a particular set of conditions. A further asymmetry is often produced by the fact that the entities governed by the reducing law are spatial parts of the entities governed by the reduced law. But this is not always the case, and cannot be treated as the source of the asymmetry in the reductive relation in general. Causal realists also anticipate that reducing theories will bring us closer to a characterisation of the mechanism, which explains the higher-level regularity.

Optimists regarding the unity of science claimed that all causal explanatory laws, at whatever level of theory, will ultimately be reduced, in conformity to this model, to the nomological regularities of physics, via the reductive identification of their kinds with kinds individuated by the explanatory theories of physics. Clearly any such project would require many intermediate stages. From psychology we would move to neuro-physiology and biology before proceeding to chemistry and physics. Mind-brain identity theorists[1] were providing an account of the relation between the mental and the physical which fitted this reductionist model. Psychological kinds were to be identified with physical kinds and consequently psychological laws derivable from physical ones. The level of physical theory concerned here would

[1] See C.V. Borst (ed.), *The Mind/Brain Identity Theory*, New York 1970.

4. Anti-reductionism and Psycho-physical laws

initially be neurophysiology. The advantages of such a strategy seems clear, for it resolves the question of how the psychological explanations of our actions are related to potential neurophysiological explanations of our movements. Such a question is urgent if we are physicalists, in the sense of accepting that changes which are physically describable can be completely explained by means of physical antecedents, governed by laws using only the vocabulary of physical science. If physicalism is true, the physical movements by means of which an agent performs an intentional act will have causal explanations in physical terms. Reductionism rules out over-determination and explains why it is that the predictions made from within each explanatory level march in step.

Reductionism also answers the arguments of those theorists who insist that we cannot take causal relations at the intentional level as 'brute'. They require vindication by the physical constitutions of the intentional systems, and such vindication must take the form of reduction.[1] Graham MacDonald bases such an argument on what he terms the principle of micro-determinism:

> What [the mental] cannot do is (non-physically) interfere in the physical causal process, nor can it causally effect other processes at the supervening level without this being mediated by the physical causes.[2]

Such a principle also seems to be what Richard Boyd has in mind when he says that our scientific practice points to 'macro-causal links being constituted out of

[1] For Colin McGinn (1980) such vindication must take the form of the discovery of essences for our natural kinds which bestow metaphysical necessity on our causal laws. It is not clear, however, that this demand is met even within our favoured physical theories.

[2] G. MacDonald 1986, 209.

interaction of forces at the micro-level between micro-particles in which the principle of conservation of energy is maintained'.[1] For MacDonald such a principle directly yields the conclusion that 'the macro-causal laws therefore are essentially derivative from laws governing the micro-processes. Reductionism would appear to be vindicated.'[2]

These arguments for reduction will be given more attention in the following chapter, where we will need to consider how far anti-reductionist materialism can go to meet them.

4. Arguments against reduction

In recent years, however, a series of anti-reductionist arguments have been developed which lead to the rejection of the classical reductive model as applied to the relation between the mental and the physical. The most famous anti-reductionist arguments currently discussed originated in the work of Donald Davidson.[3] These arguments were presented by Davidson as arguments against the possibility of psycho-physical laws *per se*. This claim is stronger than an anti-reductionist one. For although reduction requires laws, not all law-like links amount to reduction. By such laws Davidson means those in which physical kinds are linked nomologically to psychological kinds but also laws in which psychological predicates and physical predicates are conjoined. If we are to accept that our intentional explanations are causal explanations, we need to assume that laws of the latter kind are possible. As Davidson points out, the mental

[1] Boyd 1984a.

[2] G. MacDonald 1986, 209.

[3] Davidson 1980, essays 11-13, and Vermazen & Hintikka 1985, 'Replies' to essays 10-12.

does not constitute a closed system. Too much affects the mental which is not by any obvious criterion mental. Moreover the conditions which are needed for our intentional states to bring about action are often physical conditions, without psychological or intentional properties. If Davidson's arguments are successful, not only in resisting reduction but in ruling out psycho-physical laws of any kind, we must reject a causal explanatory account of the intentional. In what follows we must therefore consider whether we can accept his anti-reductionist arguments without concluding that no kind of psycho-physical law is possible.

Davidson's argument rests on the *constitutive role of rationality* in the assignment of intentional descriptions. He has recently put the matter thus:

> Beliefs, intentions and desires are identified by their objects, and these are identified by their logical and semantic properties. If attitudes can be identified at all, then, they must be found to be largely consistent with one another (because of their logical properties), and in line with the real world (because of their semantic properties) ... if a creature has propositional attitudes then that creature is approximately rational.[1]

If we are to assign propositional attitudes at all, we must assign them in such a way that the creature conforms to certain standards of rationality. Beliefs, for example, tend to produce other beliefs, for which they provide reasons: that is, beliefs which they deductively or inductively support. They are not causally stable in the presence of environmental conditions which count as evidence against them. In combination with desires they tend to produce actions which are ways of satisfying those desires. Desires produce other desires which they

[1] Vermazen & Hintikka 1985, 245.

regard as needed to promote their satisfaction. Moreover the explanation of an intentional action depends crucially on displaying the action to be of the kind the agent intended and for which she had reasons. Here the fact that the action was of a kind rationalised by her intentional states is the key explanatory feature (a causal explanatory feature on my account, but it is just here that Davidson would disagree).

Davidson points to two features of these constraints of rationality. First, they are applied *holistically*. It is only possible to attribute to an agent beliefs if we can also attribute desires and intentions. There are restrictions on what sets of intentional states we can co-ascribe, and which states we ascribe has consequences for how the agent is likely to behave in a whole range of different circumstances. Secondly, these constraints are *normative*. Attributions of propositional attitudes 'cannot be divorced from such questions as what constitutes a good argument, a valid experience, a rational plan, or a good reason for acting'.[1] 'We try for a theory that finds him consistent, a believer of truths and a lover of the good.'[2] In Chapter One we accepted at least this much regarding the normative nature of reason-giving links. What constitutes a reason for beliefs/desires/intentions is determined in relation to goals of truth and satisfaction. These goals are not fully attainable but form the ideal in relation to which reason-giving links are defined. These goals are themselves located within an explanatory project which regards human beings as 'environmentally integrated systems'.[3] These considerations make it difficult to see how we could characterise the essential features of the reason-giving link without consideration

[1] Davidson 1980, 241.
[2] Ibid., 222.
[3] Cf. Pettit, in McDowell & Pettit 1986.

of the normative goals and thereby how our explanations could be intelligible without a grasp of them. This last point links to Davidson's claim that the reason-giving relations which serve to define our intentional kinds 'have no echo in physical theory'.[1] Without the use of intentional vocabulary such links could not be expressed. This also seems right. It is difficult to see how we could capture our relations of providing evidence for, inductively or deductively supporting etc., without the use of intentional or semantic vocabulary for such relations are relations between intentional contents.

For Davidson these features of our intentional theory ensure its irreducibility to physical theory. It is worth looking in detail at the kind of reduction which is at issue here. Certainly there is a conceptual disparity between intentional and non-intentional predicates, but the argument extends to the irreducible nature of intentional kinds and of any generalisations in which such kinds might feature. Intentional kinds are individuated by their role in intentional theory, a role which is articulated by the attribution to them of semantic contents and the broadly logical and conceptual links between such contents. It is via these intentional links that the relations such states bear to each other and to the agent's behaviour and environment are captured. If these intentional links cannot be captured non-intentionally, there is no way in which we can provide, in physical terms, an account of what it is for a state to count as a desire or an intention. It is therefore not just our psychological predicates that are irreducible, but our psychological kinds too.

It does not seem possible to resist this argument by suggesting that intentional relations are inessential

[1] Davidson 1980, 231.

artifacts of just one mode of describing intentional kinds. For such links are essential to the *explanatory work* they do. This explanatory work has several connected aspects. Take a case where we explain, an intentional act. Our understanding of such an act depends on our viewing it as rational or appropriate given the agent's goals and beliefs. Such appropriateness can only be displayed via our intentional descriptions. For Davidson the explanatory work of our intentional descriptions rests only on making manifest the rationality of our responses. Intentional explanations are essentially justificatory, and non-intentional characterisations have no way of capturing the normative components which they require. For the causal explanatory theorist, however, things are more complex. For her intentional descriptions play not only a justificatory role. *They provide a pattern of conceptualisation which yields conditional dependencies and empirical generalisations.* Such patterns of dependencies must themselves be irreducible if the causal explanatory work of our intentional explanations is not to be captured at the physical level. The crucial point here is that such conditional and general claims are predicated on the backs of the intentional links.

Consider this example of Christopher Peacocke's:

> Peter is walking along the road because he wants to buy a paper and he believes that the shop shuts in five minutes. Someone who accepts this explanation is committed to the truth of multifarious conditionals and counterfactuals: for example ... if he has no other reason for going that way, Peter will stop walking in that direction if he notices that the shop has closed down early. It is because such conditionals and counterfactuals are required for the correctness of the explanation that such explanations have for us such predictive and explanatory power as they do ... If one did not know the contents of these attitudes of Peter's which explain his walking, one would not know

what conditional consequences his explanation would have.[1]

Our understanding of Peter's act requires a grasp of how he would have acted had things been different. It is just by considering what other actions would be appropriate that we work out the conditional implications of our intentional explanations and formulate their supporting generalisations. If the notion of appropriateness is irreducible, so must be the distinctive intelligibility it conveys to the action. Moreover, if we use intentional notions to capture our conditional claims and formulate our generalisations and these intentional links are not capturable at the physical level, we have no reason to suppose that the counterfactual and conditional links could be captured in a non-intentional way. It would be surprising if generalisations constructed on the basis of reason-giving links should have isomorphic parallels at the physical level, where such links are absent. Exactly parallel considerations apply to beliefs explained by other beliefs or via appropriate environmental conditions. Neither the relation of providing evidence for, nor the pattern of conditional dependencies captured using that notion, appear susceptible to non-intentional characterisation. The pattern of dependencies of belief is worked out by considering what, in different circumstances, it would be rational or appropriate to believe.

Without intentional notions therefore the explanatory work of our intentional kinds cannot be accommodated: and thus their irreducibility to non-intentional kinds seems assured.

This is the heart of the argument, for the irreducibility of our intentional kinds. What implications does it have for psycho-physical laws? We need to consider three

[1] Peacocke 1979b.

97

different kinds of such laws. First, there is the question of law-like *bi*-conditional links between intentional and physical kinds. Such laws are necessary (but not sufficient) for reduction. We have provided arguments which give us reason to doubt the possibility of any such bi-conditional links being law-like. The very disparate theoretical anchors of our intentional and physical conceptual schemes make it implausible to suppose that a single-kind classification from one scheme should systematically and projectibly coincide with a unique-kind classification from the other. What makes something a belief of a certain kind is its link to evidence, and to intentional acts. Environments which are physically very different can count as evidence, and behaviour physically very different can constitute the same intentional act. Physical kinds will be linked to environments characterised in terms of physical theory and behaviour characterised as physical movements, nerves firing etc. It is for just these reasons that we require intentional characterisations to capture the conditional dependencies of our intentional states. Such considerations, however, while telling against the possibility of bi-conditional psycho-physical laws do not appear to threaten the possibility of one-way law-like links between the physical and the mental. It seems quite plausible to suppose that certain arrangements of physical states could be *sufficient* to ground our intentional descriptions. Indeed the truth of materialism might seem to require this (see Chapter Five). Neither do the arguments rule out the possibility of mixed laws of a kind which a causal interpretation of our intentional explanation would require. To exclude psychological laws of either of these kinds Davidson requires more strands in his argument. The arguments against reduction are not *per se* arguments against psycho-physical laws.

5. Psycho-physical laws

The extra strand which Davidson needs in his arguments to move from anti-reductionism to rejecting psycho-physical laws is provided by the claimed indeterminacy of our intentional descriptions:

> A theory to explain a person's verbal and other behaviour requires the assignment of propositional contents to his sentences and attitudes. But where theory constrains us to draw a sharp line, only a shaded area is indicated by the evidence. Within this area there is, as Quine has insisted, no fact of the matter.[1]

Such indeterminacy, for Davidson, rules out the possibility of intentional descriptions featuring in causal laws, for a law must be such that 'while it may have provisos limiting its applications, it allows us to determine in advance whether or not the conditions of application are satisfied'.[2] Where the antecedents are intentional states, it would not be determinate (the point is not just an epistemological one), in advance of the consequent, whether or not such intentional states were present. Moreover, as the physical states of a system are fixed at any time, no assignment of physical states can be sufficient to determine an assignment of intentional states, so there can be no one-way law-like links from the physical to the mental. If such sufficiency was possible, the physical states would fix the assignment of intentional states, which would thereby be no longer indeterminate. Davidson cannot allow this, for he claims such fixing would wean our intentional descriptions away from their necessary anchorage in rationalising

[1] Vermazen & Hintikka 1985, 245.
[2] Davidson 1980, 233.

theory, and thereby amount to a change in subject matter.

There are two aspects of the operation of the constraints of rationality which, for Davidson, ensure indeterminacy. First, the constraints have implications for the total set of intentional states an agent can have at a time, but also for the pattern of such states through time. Our ascriptions of belief/desire/intention has to be done so that the total attribution through time makes the agent appear as rational as possible. As a consequence of this kind of holism later behaviour of a system forces us to modify earlier assignments of intentional states, and this modification of theory is something which can go on *without limit*. Therefore it can never be determinately true of an agent at any given time that she has certain intentional states. What intentional states an agent has, then, is never determinately fixed, and certainly not fixed in advance of any particular behaviour which we might use such a state to explain, in the way that causal explanation requires.

Secondly, the constraint of rationality is a normative constraint[1] (see above). There is, he claims, no uniquely determinate way to assign intentional states in our attempt to make a system approximate to the norms of rationality. John McDowell[2] has recently developed the Davidsonian claims that the normative constraints governing our intentional description rule out the possibility of law-like relations to the physical:

> ... it is something with the status of an ideal which is being credited with a constitutive role in governing our thinking about propositional attitudes. To recognise the ideal status of the constitutive concept is to appreciate

[1] See n. 8.
[2] McDowell 1985.

that the concepts of the propositional attitudes have their proper home in explanations of a special sort: explanations in which things are made intelligible by being revealed to be, or to approximate to being as they rationally ought to be.[1]

For McDowell as for Davidson such explanation is *sui generis* and not of a causal explanatory kind.

If we accept Davidson's conclusions we are required to adopt a view of the nature of mental states, and that of intentional explanation, which is in conflict with that offered in this book. Within this alternative picture our attribution of intentional states to a system is regarded as a 'rationalistic calculus of interpretation and prediction, an idealising ... instrumentalist interpretation method'.[2] The method is rationalist because it is constrained by the ideal of rationality, idealising because no one's behaviour conforms totally to the model set-up, and instrumentalist at least in the sense that the data which our theory describes are not sufficient to determine as true any given pattern of interpretation, and there is nothing else beyond this data which is relevant to fixing these truth values.[3] Within this framework the explanatory work done by the assignment of intentional descriptions is purely of an interpretive and justificatory kind. We render a system intelligible by showing that its behaviour can be described as approximating to that of our ideally rational agent. This was the view of intentional explanation criticised in Chapters One and

[1] Ibid., 389.

[2] Dennett 1987.

[3] Someone might think that Davidson's adoption of a token identity thesis between mental events and physical events shows him to have a realist view of mental events. His instrumentalism, however, concerns not the existence of such events but their intentional characterisation.

Two. If we reject it we need to reject Davidson's arguments.

One thing we do not need to accept from the Davidsonian picture is that the constraints of rationality have to operate in the inter-temporal way which he suggests. The constraints demand a whole range of conditional dependencies, of intentional states on each other, on the environment, and of potential behaviour on intentional states. These however are conditional truths which could be true of an agent at a time. Rather than accept that later behaviour can force us to modify descriptions applied earlier, I suggest that we view these constraints as making claims which are about the dispositions which the agent has *at the time* at which certain intentional descriptions are true of her, and the conditional dependencies between them. If we dislike the implication that dispositional claims can be 'barely true', we must look to the categorical physical states of the agent, in combination with environment circumstances, to ground these dispositional claims. This would clearly make demands of the agent's physical states, but it would need argument to claim that they couldn't provide such a grounding. Within this account later behaviour will only be relevant as evidence for what these earlier dispositions were. It will not, in itself, be determining. If the constraints are viewed in this way they do not provide an obstacle to the possibility of an agent's intentional states being determinate at some time t, prior to her acting intentionally, in the same way that her physical states are. It is only if we ignore such inner physical states and assume that our intentional descriptions are only answerable to (make demands of) our behaviour, that the position that we need to wait for later behaviour to determine the assignment of intentional descriptions to some earlier state seems plausible.

102

4. Anti-reductionism and Psycho-physical laws

If we allow the physical to play a role in grounding our intentional descriptions, have we thereby weaned such descriptions away from their proper home within intentional theory? No. To argue that our physical states might ground our intentional descriptions is distinct from making a reductive claim (see Chapter Five). If physical states can be sufficient for the truth of intentional descriptions, such sufficiency must relate a physical base and intentional states as presently individuated. To do otherwise would indeed be to change the subject. Accepting law-like links is not to give the physical characteristics authority in respect of whether or not a certain intentional state is present. Such laws could only be constructed via the recognition that where certain physical descriptions were true we could also truly ascribe intentional descriptions, anchored, as at present, within intentional theory. (More on this in Chapter Six.) If there appeared to be a clash between the physical base mentioned in a putative law and our intentional criteria this would simply disprove the supposed law.

If we reject the inter-temporal operation of the principles of rationality we reject one argument for the lack of determinacy of an agent's intentional states. What then are we to make of the claim that the normative nature of our rationalising ascriptions, their implicit reference to an ideal, threatens their determinacy and/or their causal explanatory role? How is the *ideal* featuring in such explanation? It is true that to grasp what counts as rational connections between beliefs we have to grasp the ideal of beliefs being true. Similarly in the practical case, we need to grasp the ideal in relation to which an agent wishes to construct her choices, to judge which choices are rational for her (see above). In each of these cases the fact that these judgments of rationality are made in relation to an ideal does not serve to make what is judged non-factual in a way that undermines the possibility of its playing a role in causal explanation. (Whether an edge is straight is judged in relation to a non-instantiable ideal, but none the less often has important causal consequences.) It is, of course, the case that intentional explanations in these areas point to and depend on the rationalising links. What does not follow is that these rationalising links cannot be playing a causal explanatory role. If my desire is to be explained (and not simply justified) by its constituting a rational response to my situation, the fact that it constitutes such a response must, on the view defended in this book, be causally relevant to its occurrence. Nothing in McDowell's claim that in characterising what such rationality consists in we have to grasp what would constitute an ideally rational agent, seems to undermine that view.

6. Conclusion

Arguments which establish that mental (construed as intentional) kinds cannot be reduced to physical kinds do not necessarily rule out psycho-physical laws, and therefore do not necessarily rule out causal explanation at the intentional level. Further arguments against psycho-physical laws can be resisted. If we accept the anti-reductionist arguments, however, and wish to be materialists, we are faced with the task of characterising a form of materialism which is compatible with anti-reductionism and considering whether such materialism is sufficient to vindicate causal explanatory claims at the intentional level, and can go some way to accommodate the motivations of those who argue for a reductionist position.

CHAPTER FIVE

Supervenience and Reduction

1. Supervenience

In the previous chapter I suggested that it is possible to defend a causal explanatory view of intentional kinds and to be a materialist without accepting the reduction of intentional kinds or laws to physical ones. It is now time to turn direct attention to the kind of materialism compatible with this set of assumptions. The adoption of a materialist stance is not something I will defend directly. I am rather investigating the coherence of a set of positions, and materialism is one component of that set. Given the causal explanatory role assigned in this book to our intentional descriptions, the form of materialism adopted must be compatible with realism about such descriptions. It is not possible to regard them as mere devices for systematising behaviour (Instrumentalism). Rather they must be regarded as true or false of the agents which they describe; moreover the truth or falsity of certain intentional descriptions must be determined in advance of the behaviour which they are invoked to explain. In previous chapters we have noted ways in which we might need the physical to support our explanations at the intentional level. Our intentional claims carry with them complex implications regarding the dispositions of an agent at the time at which certain intentional descriptions are true of her. If we are unhappy with the suggestion that dispositional claims can be barely true, we need some categorical groundings which can make such claims true. We therefore look for a form of materialism which can satisfy that demand.

Within current literature non-reductive materialism is characterised in terms of supervenience.[1] Our immediate aim, therefore, must be to examine the relation of supervenience, inspect its anti-reductionist credentials and consider whether it can satisfy the needs we have articulated in a way compatible with causal explanation at the intentional level.

The claim that psychological states of affairs are supervenient on physical states of affairs might be expressed as the claim that the physical facts, those described by our fundamental physical theories, are the facts *in virtue of which*[2] all true descriptions of the world are true. To express the supervenience claim in this way is to construe supervenience as an ontological relation between properties, and not simply an indiscernibility relation between predicates. Supervenience in the latter sense would simply be the claim that no entities could differ in the psychological predicates which attached to them, without also differing in the physical predicates which attached to them. Such supervenience could be accepted by those who do not accept a realist view of the supervening level of description (in this case the mental). The indiscernibility claim would then be defended via considerations of proper or consistent projection of the supervening descriptions.[3] For someone who is committed to causal explanatory work of higher level

---

[1] See C. & G. MacDonald 1987.

[2] I adopt this term from Hartry Field 1975.

[3] See Klagge 1988.

properties, however, such anti-realist moves are not available. Rather the supervenience relation is interpreted as a relation of ontological determination and dependency between properties, the reality of each of which is accepted, but where the base properties are regarded as more fundamental.

Supervenience can be thought of as a relation between families of properties, in this case the mental and the physical. It can then be conceived of *globally*. Any world which is like this world in every physical respect will be like it in every mental respect. However, we are frequently interested in relations of supervenience of a more local kind, in which we identify more precisely the more fundamental descriptions in virtue of which higher-level claims are true. In the mental/physical case we must be interested in these localised claims of dependency, as well as the global ones, for we are concerned mutually to accommodate causal explanations at the psychological and physiological levels. There are many examples of such localised supervenience claims outside of the psycho-physical case:

(a) 'The dish is fragile' may be true in virtue of the dish being made of glass, or of its being made of china;

(b) 'A signalled' may be true in virtue of A putting her arm out of the window of her car (given certain conventions governing signalling);

(c) 'Britain entered the war' may be true in virtue of Parliament making a declaration, armies being mobilised, given certain directives, etc.

These examples suggest the following sets of conditions to be characteristic of the supervenience relation:

If on a particular occasion, S_1 is true in virtue of the

truth of S_2 (the state of affairs described by S_1 supervenient on the state of affairs described by S_2)[1] then:

(a) The truth of S_2 is *in general* sufficient for the truth of S_1. Such sufficiency may be dependent on the kinds of circumstances in which S_2 is found. Putting an arm out of a car window is sufficient for signalling only in certain contexts. The supervenience relation therefore requires the truth of certain law-like generalisations which reflect such sufficiency.[2] Whenever S_2 is true and C is true, then S_1 is true; e.g. whenever a dish is made of a certain kind of glass, it will be fragile. These generalisations may include ineliminable *ceteris paribus* clauses. In terms of our examples we may be able to imagine further circumstances which would make it clear that A's arm movement was not signalling, or which would frustrate Britain's entry into the war, without being able to find a general characterisation of all such possible circumstances to insert into the general law.

(b) The truth of S_1 need not, however, be *in general* sufficient for the truth of S_2. On different occasions S_1 may be true in virtue of the truth of distinct sentences (a different dish may be fragile because it is made of porcelain).

(c) However *on each particular occasion* the truth of S_1 is sufficient for the truth of S_2, i.e. *S_2 is necessary for S_1.* The kind of necessity involved here is necessity in the particular circumstances. Excluding cases where there are two distinct states of affairs, each sufficient for the truth of S_1, if S_1 is supervenient on S_2 then the counterfactual circumstances in which S_2 is not true are circumstances in which S_1 is not true either.

These conditions are intended to capture modal

[1] S_1 and S_2 here are sentence types.
[2] See Kim 1978.

features of the supervenience relation. Such formal features, however, are not sufficient to capture the relation with which materialists have been concerned: namely, a relation of non-causal necessitation and dependency between the physical and the psychological, which falls short of reduction. The modal characterisation of this relation leaves several key issues unclarified. One issue concerns the nature of the necessity involved. It is physical, logical, metaphysical? What is the range of the necessity? Another thing we need to know is what distinguishes the relation of supervenience from that of causation. We also need to know on what grounds supervenience can be termed a materialist relation. What is to justify us in giving ontological priority to the supervening base? Finally we need to consider whether we can sustain the claim that the relation of supervenience is distinct from that of reduction.

The relation which is illustrated by our examples seems quite different from the causal relation, at least as this is ordinarily conceived. The states of affairs linked by supervenience do not appear sufficiently distinct for the relation between them to be a causal one. Moreover if this relation is to be used to characterise materialism, it must be distinguished from the causal relation. For many dualists would accept that psychological states of affairs were causally dependent on physical ones. One obvious suggestion would be that the sufficiency involved in the supervenience relation is logical or conceptual. But this does not seem applicable to all cases. The fact that the dish is made of glass does not entail that it is fragile. If this is correct, the relation of supervenience involves a sufficiency that is neither *causal* nor always *logical*.

What then distinguishes causation and supervenience? We cannot always evoke temporal asymmetry. Causes normally precede their effects, but if we take the case of a weight on a cushion causing an indentation in the cushion, it is not clear that temporal precedence is necessary for causation.[1] Moreover some cases of supervenience require circumstances which may temporally precede the supervening states of affairs. Links of supervenience, however, though not conceptual truths, are links which are dictated by our conceptual scheme. This bestows on them a necessity which though *a posteriori* is stronger than what we normally require of causal links. Consider the case in which our description of a room in terms of macro-objects is supervenient on its description in terms of certain kinds of molecules at certain space-time points. The former description, though supervenient on the latter, is not derivable from it. Faced with an instantiation of the latter description, however, descriptions in terms of tables, chairs etc. would be forced on us, and forced on us by our concepts of such macro-objects. It would not be possible for the molecular states of affairs to exist without the state of affairs involving tables and chairs to exist. The impossibility here seems of a different order from that of an effect failing to follow its cause. It may be appropriate to call it metaphysical.

Kim[2] draws a distinction between weak and strong supervenience. Weak supervenience is relativised to worlds. There is no possible world in which two events (objects, states) *in that world* share their physical properties and differ in their mental properties. Strong supervenience does not share such relativisation and claims that where events (objects, states) share their

---

[1] If we can argue for the temporal precedence of the cause here then causality may be distinguished from supervenience, in that causally sufficient conditions temporally precede their consequent.

[2] Kim 1984/5.

physical properties they also share their mental properties. Within the ontological interpretation of supervenience however it seems to be strong supervenience which we require, for 'weak supervenience of the mental on the physical is compatible with there being a world just like the actual world in every physical respect, but in which no mental events occur'.[1]

What justifies us in giving ontological priority to the supervening base? In the mental/physical case how are we to justify the claim that the physical descriptions are more fundamental, a claim needed if accepting supervenience gives us materialist credentials? Such priority cannot be guaranteed from the lack of general necessitation from the mental descriptions to physical ones. This is a reflection of a range of possible supervenient bases for our mental descriptions, a characteristic which will be important when we distinguish supervenience from reduction, but which is not itself sufficient to yield materialism. Indeed the asymmetry which is at issue here is just what the relation of supervenience (in its strong sense) shares with reduction, and so it cannot be constituted out of the absence of bi-conditional links. One of the things which is important is the defence given to the claim that the supervening base is necessary in the circumstances for the supervenient description to hold. Such defence originates in the materialist assumption that mental states cannot exist without physical states. (Parallel assumptions in the other examples would be that dispositions must be grounded, and that social facts cannot exist without individuals etc.) This is related to a feature which we attended to in the case of reduction, justifying the claim that the reducing base is more

[1] McLaughlin in Lepore & McLaughlin 1985, 366.

fundamental than the base reduced. The material properties which in particular arrangements and circumstances form a supervenient base (or reductive base) for our psychological descriptions can be found in other circumstances and arrangements without any attendant mental properties. This seems to justify the claim that they are not dependent for their existence on the mental; a claim not available to us in the reverse direction.

2. Supervenience vs. reduction

Supervenience is claimed to be a relation of dependency which is distinct from that of reduction. What is the distinction? Initially the answer seems clear. Even if we accept that the supervenience relation requires nomological links, these appear to be only one way, from the base to the supervening properties or states of affairs. Reduction required bi-conditional links, necessary co-extensiveness between kinds at each level of description. This apparent difference may however be challenged. For example, in the intentional case supervenience holds that the instantiation of intentional properties always requires some physical descriptions to be true. It might then be thought that the different physical bases grounding a given psychological kind could be formed into a disjunction. It would then be the case that there would be bi-conditional links between intentional and physical kinds, as in cases of reduction. It would simply be that the physical kind was a disjunctive kind. If such a move was accepted it could be extended to the reduction of intentional laws. The physical laws governing the supervenience bases of intentional kinds could be formed into a disjunction and laws at the intentional level derived from them.[1] In the face of such a possibility can we still maintain that supervenience is a relation which is distinct from reduction?

One point which is important in this connection was made in the last chapter. Reduction requires more than bi-conditional links and the derivation of laws. It is not a relation which can be captured solely by attention to modal links. These do not, for example, illustrate the asymmetry such a relation requires. Moreover it was claimed that for reduction to be achieved the explanatory work at the reduced level must be matched at the reducing level. In the intentional case the irreducibility of notions of *appropriateness, making rational,* etc. ensured the irreducibility of our intentional kinds, even if bi-conditional links were to be found. However, for the causal explanatory theorist such notions provided not a *sui generis* model of intelligibility for intentional action but a pattern of conceptualisation which yielded conditional dependencies and empirical generalisations. Such patterns of dependency must themselves be irreducible if the causal explanatory work of our intentional explanations is not be be captured at the physical level. Granted that any justificatory work of our intentional kinds is not captured by the postulated disjunctions, is the causal explanatory work?

Some writers[2] have made the point that the number of different physical kinds which could ground an intentional kind may be infinite. Reduction could then only proceed if we were prepared to accept a possibly infinite disjunction on the reducing side. The issue of whether the disjunctive set on the reducing side is finite or infinite, however, does not appear to be the most important. Infinite sets can be constructed in principled

[1] See Kim 1978.
[2] E.g. Putnam 1988, 78.

and projectible ways. What is important is what kind of *unity* the set can be taken to possess. What was characteristic of classical reduction was that higher-level properties were reduced to properties which formed a natural kind at the reducing level, kinds, which at that level had their own criteria of individuation and fitted into a body of explanatory theory. Such a kind seems quite different from a mere *list* of all the physical states on which an intentional kind happens to supervene. The crucial question is whether such a list, finite or infinite, has a unifying characterisation in terms of physical theory, a characterisation which fits into a body of laws and explanations, or whether the unity which the disjunct possesses is via the fact that each is sufficient for a psychological description. If it is the latter, it would be our psychological classifications, applied via the criteria which we presently employ, which would decide membership of the set. Parallel considerations apply to the putative derivation of the laws from a disjunction of physical laws, and illustrate the point that reduction requires more than derivation. Where we need higher-level classifications to unify the disjunctive lower-level kinds, or disjunctive lower-level laws, it would be quite inappropriate to speak of reduction. If this is right, we have a further condition to add to those required for the reduction of kinds, and their corresponding generalisations where they are kinds which fit into causal laws. Genuine reduction is only achieved when the putatively reducing kind forms a natural kind at its own level of theory, fitting into a body of explanatory theory at that level, and correspondingly when the body of laws from which any higher-level laws are derived are themselves part of a unified body of theory. In each case the issue is whether *explanatory unity* is maintained at the reducing level. Where it fails we have relations of supervenience, not reduction. This condition, of course, is a further articulation of the requirement that reduction only occurs when explanatory work is maintained at the reducing level. Where supervenience holds we will, in principle, have a derivation of the higher-level laws from a (sometimes infinite) disjunction of lower-level ones, but such derivation will not be equivalent to reduction.

The question of whether we have relations of reduction or supervenience is obviously one which confronts us in many areas of discourse, for example in considering the relation of the social to the psychological or the biological[1] to the physico-chemical. In the case with which we are concerned, the psychological and the physical, we have *a priori* arguments, deriving from the constraints of rationality which render at least implausible the projectible unification in physical terms of the set of physical states on which our intentional characteristics supervene. These were the arguments rehearsed in the last chapter. It is clearly an interesting question for investigation, whether in other cases too there are *a priori* considerations suggesting the plasticity of supervening kinds with relation to their base.[2]

If we accept the distinction between supervenience and reduction, we can utilise the notion of supervenience to articulate a materialism compatible with the anti-reductionist arguments put forward in the last chapter.

---

[1] This might be an example from biology. Imagine that we explain the colour of a butterfly's wings by the fact that it fits the butterfly for the environment. Maybe also that colour is explicable in terms of the biochemical make-up of the wings. Different butterflies might be of different colours, each dependent on distinct biochemical constituents. To remain at the biochemical level, however, would be to miss something which is strikingly informative at the biological level: namely, that each butterfly is coloured in a way that fits it for its environment.

[2] See G. MacDonald 1986.

In postulating a relation of supervenience between psychological and physical kinds we have a materialist thesis which allows a realist construal of mental descriptions. The physical states which form the base for our intentional descriptions can provide the categorical base for the dispositional claims such descriptions imply. To see the relation in terms of supervenience rather than reduction, however, is to accept the possibility of distinct kinds at the physical level grounding one kind at the intentional level.

3. Supervenience and token identity

How does materialism, characterised in terms of supervenience, relate to other forms of materialist theses? If we accept its distinction from reductive claims it is clearly weaker than a type/type identity thesis. What is much less commonly accepted is that materialism could be true without requiring the truth of token/token identity theories, but if materialism is captured by supervenience, this also seems possible. Token/token identity theories claim that each mental particular, whether object, event or state, be identical with a particular or set of particulars picked out by means of the system of classification employed by our fundamental physical theory. For many theorists the acceptance of such token identity claims is viewed as a minimal requirement of any materialist thesis. However, it appears that supervenience could be true without its being the case that the token particulars quantified over or referred to within our psychological theories be identical with the particulars or sets of particulars quantified over or referred to in those physical descriptions on which our psychological descriptions supervene. For our classification into particulars is a function of the theory in terms of which we are describing the world. We cannot suppose that the classification which one theory yields will correspond neatly with the classification yielded by another. Some analogies may make this clearer. The state of affairs of Britain entering the war supervenes on the state of affairs of Parliament making a declaration, and the army being mobilised etc. Moreover these latter states of affairs are supervenient on certain people voting in certain ways, receiving messages and moving from place to place, and these states of affairs are supervenient on certain physical particles going through certain physical changes. In none of these instances of supervenience can we easily *identify* the particulars at one level of description with the particulars at another. This does not, however, invalidate the claims of supervenience, nor lead us to the conclusion that Britain, Parliament, the army, individual people or messages fail to exist.

Here is an example of John Haugeland's[1] concerning particular events.

> Suppose you and I each make a single-crested wave, starting from opposite ends of a swimming pool ... [which] ... hit the same cork at the same time ... At the level of description of waves hitting corks, these are quite distinct events with entirely different causal histories and correspondingly different counterfactual properties ... when we turn up our microscope, however ... there isn't a trace of a wave-hit to be found ... [just] ... some 'complex' of enormously many ... positions and velocities of water molecules.

They are certainly not distinguishable into distinct sets for each wave.

If we reject the requirement of token identity between

[1] Haugeland 1982.

mental and physical particulars as a condition of the truth of materialism, we also rid ourselves of certain problems. If we allow as a mental particular anything that is quantified over, or referred to in our true psychological descriptions, we seem committed to the existence of, for example, red after-images. In the past this has been an embarrassment for materialists, for even if we could find a plausible physical particular with which to identify the after-image, it is very unlikely that it would be red. Such a problem has led some philosophers to try to paraphrase[1] sentences with apparent references of this kind into sentences without such ontological commitments. Within materialism characterised in terms of supervenience, however, we are under no constraint to give up our belief in red after-images simply because we can find no physical particulars with which to identify them. Giving up the requirement of token identity also frees us from problematic considerations regarding essential properties. It seems an essential property of even a token pain that it is a pain, of even a token thought that it has a certain content. Yet it is difficult to see how these could be essential properties of any physical particular.

4. Physicalist arguments for reduction

To accept multiple realisation of intentional kinds, and yet to argue for their status as natural kinds, kinds occurring in causal explanatory generalisations, is to resist the suggestion that all 'higher-level' generalisations must be vindicated, in a strong way by the laws of our fundamental physical theories. In the last chapter we considered arguments which purport to show the

[1] See, however, Frank Jackson 1980, for doubts about paraphrase as a mode of ridding of us such commitments.

unsatisfactoriness of such a position. These come from within a framework which is not only materialist, but physicalist (the thesis that physical changes can be completely explained by means of physical antecedents governed by laws using only the vocabulary of physical science). The truth of physicalism is independent of the truth of ontological materialism for: (a) if we believed that mental states constituted a realm of existence distinct from the physical, we might still adopt physicalism. This would simply be the claim that reference to mental states was not needed in the causal explanations of any physically characterised movement; (b) if we accept supervenience, physicalism might none the less be false:[1] for it might still be the case that the only way in which we could explain certain physical movements would be by considering which intentional acts were performed by them, which intentional states were supervenient on their antecedents, and then utilising psychological laws linking the phenomena thus described. The ontological dependence of the psychological on the physical does not settle at what level of description the explanatory laws operate.

Most materialists, however, would also accept physicalism. Indeed the latter forms one of our governing methodological principles within science, and it will not be my purpose here to challenge it. If physicalism is true then we need an account of the connection between the physical causal antecedents of our bodily movements and the psychological causal antecedents of the intentional acts performed by those movements. If we are to avoid over-determinism there must be conditional interdependencies between the causal conditions cited in the physical and psychological explanations. More precisely:

---

[1] If physicalism were false, however, we might lose one of our reasons for believing in supervenience.

(a) The intentional antecedents of any intentional act must be sufficient in the circumstances for a limited range of physical states, linked by physical law to bodily movements by which the intentional act can be performed. (b) The physical antecedents of the bodily movements by which an intentional act is performed must be sufficient in the circumstances for the intentional states which produce those acts. Although reductive identification of the causal explanatory features at the physical and psychological level would clearly be one way in which these conditions could be satisfied, it doesn't seem required. Relations of supervenience between such features would yield the required conditions on a *case-by-case* basis.

What however are we to make of the claims of those who argue that all macro-causal links need to be vindicated by causal links at the micro-level? Here it is important to be clear whether the demand pertains to causal relations between types or tokens. For those who are impressed by a certain kind of causal realism nomological regularities linking kinds require the backing of something akin to a causal mechanism to explain them. If such a mechanism is to vindicate the law then it must be present whenever the law is instantiated. Such a demand would require reduction. However we need not accept causal realism in such a form and can rather accept autonomous causal explanatory links between higher-level kinds. To do this, we do not have to reject the claim that each *token* causal inter-action is constituted out of inter-action of forces at the micro-level. Where relations of supervenience hold, higher-level causal connections can be grounded in, or mediated by, connections at the lower level, in ways which pose no difficulty for the principle of conservation of energy. On every particular occasion on which there is a causal connection between an intentional state and an intentional act, this connection will be grounded in a physical causal connection between, for example, neurophysiological states and bodily movements. However, the same kind of intentional causal connection could supervene on distinct physical causal connections on different occasions. It is, of course, the case that supervenience carries with it some, in principle, derivation of the higher-level laws from a possibly infinite set of lower-level ones, but as we have seen above, this does not necessarily amount to reduction.

There is a further objection.[1] This says that although we can accommodate the needs of micro-determinism, and avoid the problem of over-determination, on a *case-by-case* basis, by the thesis of supervenience, we are left with a problem at the level of laws. The objection can be put like this. In the absence of reduction what grounds have we for assuming that the laws at the psychological and the physical level will march in step? If there can be many different physical realisations of a given mental kind, what guarantee can we have that the physical states which form the base for the antecedent of a law will be connected by physical laws to physical consequents which will ground the consequents of the psychological law? Without reduction, it is claimed we could have no such guarantee, and consequently no reason for accepting the projectability of our psychological laws.

One move to make in response to this objection is to point out that it is a condition of a physical system realising intentional states at all that its physical states be such that our intentional generalisations come out true. In this sense for every system (or rather for every

---

[1] Papineau 1985.

system in given environments) there is an explanation of *how* it is, for that system that our intentional generalisations project. This story may however be different for different systems. To ask for a further guarantee as to the projectability of our higher-level generalisations, in terms of vindication by lower-level laws, is to ask for just the kind of reduction which is at issue. For it is to require that higher-level laws be explicable by lower-level ones in a stronger sense that the disjunctive derivability which supervenience allows. It is that demand that the anti-reductionist claims is resistible. This is not to say that our intentional laws have no justification. They are embedded within a theory which has been successfully used to explain and predict behaviour from time immemorial and governs all of our everyday interactions with others and understanding of ourselves. But such a justification is provided within their own terminology and at their own level of description.

5. Conclusion

The causal explanatory theorist who is an anti-reductionist therefore accepts intentional kinds as natural kinds, but argues that natural kinds at one level of description need not be reducible to natural kinds at some other level, even where this further level may be ontologically more fundamental. A consequence of such a position is that if we were to abandon our psychological mode of classification we would both lose a way of grouping together states, which in terms of our physical theory are distinct, and lose a way of capturing law-like generalisations which transcend those expressible in purely physical vocabulary. Thereby we would lose a way of capturing some of the real structural features of the world.

CHAPTER SIX

Functionalism

1. What is functionalism?

⌐Materialism characterised in terms of supervenience requires neither type/type nor token/token identity theories. In recent years however it has been argued that such materialism, when combined with a realist view of the mental, and a causal explanatory account of intentional explanation, requires the truth of functionalism, and it is this claim which must now be explored. ⌐

According to the functionalist theory of the mind, to say that an agent is in some mental state, for example, believing p, is just to say that they are in *some* state which plays a specified causal role in determining their response to their environment. In the words of Brian Loar, 'to interpret the system of beliefs and desires as a functional theory is to explicate an ascription of an attitude to X in terms of X's being in a state which realises a functional role associated by the system with that form of ascription'.[1] The notion of 'explicate' which Loar is using here is a strongly reductive one. Functionalist theorists of this kind aim to tell us what it really is to be in certain intentional states. They aim to give the essence of our intentional kinds in functional

[1] Loar 1981, 10.

123

terms. Given the location of our intentional kinds within networks of intentional relations such functionalists therefore seek functional equivalents for our intentional descriptions. Explication is used in a way that suggests definitional equivalence (At the least it requires reduction of intentional kinds to functional ones.)

(The causal relations of states to each other as well as to environmental conditions and behavioural output all form part of their functional role.) For any mental ascriptions to be true there needs to be some state of the agent which plays the specified functional role, and when this state is discovered it is said to realise the agent's mental state. Most functionalists are materialists and assume that the realising states will be physical. On such an account the relation between mental and physical descriptions has the structure of existential quantification and particular instance.

In attempting to give a functionalist characterisation of psychological kinds it is clear that we cannot specify the causal role of one psychological state independently of reference to others. Virtually any belief could yield any behaviour if found with an appropriate set of other beliefs and desires. One physical state cannot alone realise one psychological state. It can only do so within a system which realises a whole psychological theory. However, if we accept that our psychological states are defined implicitly by their role within such a theory, it might be claimed that reference to each of them can be replaced in the theory by a variable. The demand which the theory makes of a system to which it applies can then be reduced to an existential claim to the effect that the system has some set of states related to each other in the way the theory specifies for its variables. It is in such a holistic way that functionalists envisage a functionalist reduction of intentional descriptions. Any such description would then be instantiated by a physical system which has a set of states counterfactually interdependent in the way specified.

If a functionalist account of intentional kinds is possible, it would provide an account of how supervenience could be true. For, according to functionalists such as Loar, we need a theory which 'explicates propositional attitude ascriptions so that they are satisfiable by purely physical systems, entirely by virtue of physical properties'. A functionalist theory of intentional states is, Loar claims, explicative in just this way, for 'it assigns to each sentence containing a theoretical term of the theory (i.e. a psychological term) an equivalent sentence, free of theoretical terms that somehow captures a functional role'.[1] This brings to the fore a central feature of those functionalist theories which I shall be considering, namely: *the functionalist descriptions which explicate our psychological descriptions must be manifestly descriptions which physical states can satisfy, and this means that the causal properties which are invoked in a functional characterisation must be describable in theory-neutral, non-psychological, non-intentional vocabulary.*

In the light of our previous discussion it is clear that this requires that the constraints of rationality governing our intentional theory must themselves be captured in non-intentional, functional terms. It is only thus that we shall have an overall account which will make explicit how the truth of certain physical descriptions is sufficient for the truth of certain psychological descriptions. Should such a condition be satisfied, then following their functionalist explication our psychological descriptions would be simply derivable from physical descriptions

[1] Ibid., 3 and 10.

given the background physical theories. This task is most fully completed where the relation of explication is that of definitional equivalence; but where explication yields only reduction of kinds, not of predicates, we will still have rendered transparent the way in which physical systems can instantiate intentional properties.

Such a project of functionalist explication needs to be distinguished from one which I shall term functionalist construction (certain work within artificial intelligence might be interpreted as a project of the latter kind). Here an attempt is made to construct a system, with a certain functional organisation, which can be described using (at least parts of) intentional theory. Such an attempt makes no claim to explicate our intentional kinds functionally. Should it be successful, it would serve to make materialism intelligible only by constructing a physical system, with a certain kind of functional organisation, which merits intentional characterisation. This might suggest that a system's functional properties are of key importance in its forming a base for intentional descriptions. This is already a plausible claim, for if we replace some physical part of our brain with a part with a distinct physico-chemical make-up which none the less plays the same role within our neurophysiological organisation, our intentional characteristics can remain the same.[1] However, this does not require us to reduce intentionality to extensional functional organisation, nor to claim that all intentional systems must have the same theory-neutral functional characterisation. Indeed, it would allow that there may be functional differences in the organisation of different intentional systems. Within the constructionist framework the relation between intentional description and functional organisation is

[1] See, for example, the case of L-Dopa in Sacks 1976.

one of supervenience. By contrast the functionalist accounts which I shall be considering in this chapter suggest that the relation is that of the strongest form of reduction.

2. Arguments for functionalist reduction

It has seemed to many writers that, given the failure of classical reduction, with psychological kinds reduced to categorical physical kinds, a realist materialism requires the truth of functionalism. The force of these arguments derives from a list of conditions which it seems any satisfactory materialist theory of the mind must satisfy. It is then claimed that functionalism is the only way of satisfying these conditions. (This is the argument adopted for example by Brian Loar in the first chapter of *Mind and Meaning*.)[1]

The intelligibility condition

If we accept ontological materialism, and, therefore, supervenience, it may seem reasonable to require that we should make intelligible how it is that our psychological descriptions are made true by physical states. Without some account of the mental to suggest how this is possible the relation remains brute and mysterious. Functionalism provides such intelligibility by explicating our psychological descriptions in a way that makes manifest how physical systems can instantiate them (see above). This feature of functionalism provides one of the strongest arguments in its favour. Indeed it provides the main motivation for reductive functionalism. The aim is to tell us what

[1] Loar, 1981.

intentional states really are in a way that shows how they can be materially realised.⟩

Within the functionalist model the relation between intentional kinds and functional kinds is one of reduction, and the relation between such functional kinds and what might be termed categorical physical kinds, that of supervenience. This is because most functionalists accept multiple realisation.⟦The physical states playing a given functional role may be different on different occasions. This is the advantage that functionalism has over traditional type/type identity theories. On each occasion however the relation between the functional and physical kind will be perspicuous.⟧For in each case it will have the structure of existential quantification and particular instance. Such a theory would then yield the law-like conditionals between the physical base and the supervening mental properties which supervenience requires via an intermediary functional vocabulary.

⟨ *The demarcation condition* ⟩

An account of the mental must provide a criterion which marks off those systems which can be attributed psychological states from those which cannot. The criterion must be spelt out in such a way as to make explicit the claims which intentional descriptions make of any agent to which they are applied, to distinguish correct and incorrect applications of them, and also in a way which explains how these claims can come to be understood, by those who have mastery of our intentional theory.

From the instrumentalist perspective a creature has intentional states just in case 'its behaviour and perceptual circumstances can successfully be systematised'[1] by the ascription of such states (plus some further conditions to rule out triviality). If, however, we want to reject instrumentalism and accept that our mental descriptions make demands of our *inner states*, then functionalism provides an appropriate demarcation condition:

A functionalist interpretation of the belief-desire theory yields a demarcation condition quite straightforwardly. X has desires and beliefs provided that X is functionally organised in such and such a way and X actually is in some of the states defined by that functional organisation.[2]

The need for explanatory vindication

Once we accept physicalism, and thereby accept that sufficient physical causal conditions can be found for our bodily movements, if we wish to retain our intentional theories we need an account of the relation between the psychological and the physical antecedents of action, which ensures that our intentional explanations are *vindicated*, not replaced. That is, we want the relation between the psychological and the physical explanations to support the explanatory claims made at the psychological level, as true and justified, rather than simply provide an alternative explanatory theory at the physical level which is both more successful and displays our psychological explanatory claims to be misguided,

---

[1] Ibid., 14.

[2] Ibid. It is not the case that the only facts on which a demarcation condition might make demands are either the behaviour, or inner states of a system. Psychological descriptions can supervene on a much wider range of facts about the world and our social group. The implications of this will be discussed in the next chapter.

and therefore to be abandoned.⌉The reason we look for vindication rather than replacement is that our psychological explanatory claims are central to what we take to be distinctive of us as persons and govern all our everyday interactions with one another. In this respect they have been very successfully tested. A functionalist account, it has been argued, provides for such vindication.⌈For such theorists, at the psychological level of explanation, we claim that a certain behavioural effect was caused by a state which also had a range of other causal properties. This claim is vindicated if, at the physical level of description, we are provided with a physical state producing the bodily movement with just the range of causal properties specified. ⌋

It is important to note, however, that for most functionalists such vindication is only provided on a case-by-case basis. In this way it is similar to the vindication provided by supervenience claims. Because most functionalists accept multiple realisation, intentional generalisations, which they regard as fully reducible to functional generalisations, are unlikely to be further reducible to non-functional physical laws. In previous chapters we have considered arguments requiring the reduction of higher-level causal explanatory laws. Were such arguments cogent they would tell against functional laws as much as against intentional laws. This makes it clear that the arguments for functionalist reduction are quite distinct from these previously considered arguments for physicalist reduction. There the concern was to provide a physical mechanism for our intentional causal connections, and a physical justification for the projectibility of higher-level laws. The primary concern was such explanatory vindication. The functionalists' motivation for reduction is primarily ontological. They aim to show how intentional states can supervene on physical states.

3. Problems with functionalist reduction

⌈Within functionalist theories psychological states are defined in terms of their causal roles. These roles include their relations to environmental conditions, behaviour and other psychological states. The key claim of such theories as I have outlined them is that these roles must be capturable in non-intentional vocabulary. This is the source of the problems with the theory. Specification of the conditional dependencies of our intentional states as embodied in our psychological theories makes ineliminable reference to the intentional content of those states and to the conceptual and logical links between the characterisation of such contents and the descriptions of the system's environment and behaviour. The anti-reductionist arguments articulated in Chapter Four have direct application here. Such intentional links cannot be captured non-intentionally. ⌉

Functionalists have been aware of the challenge presented by such considerations, and have tried in various ways to meet it. Common to these suggestions is the view that intentionality is an incidental feature of our psychological kinds, rather than an essential individuating condition of them. One suggestion, which has taken different forms, is the adoption of a *syntactic* theory of the mind. Recognising the difficulty of providing extensional, functional explications of states with semantic content, such a theory recommends the development of a contentless psychology whose classificatory kinds can be explicated in the way the functionalist requires. One theorist who has suggested the development of a syntactic theory of mind is Stephen Stich.[1] A key question for any such theory concerns how

[1] Stich 1983; see also Paul Churchland 1981 and 1984, and Patricia Smith Churchland 1980.

131

we relate the new, purely functionally characterised kinds of our contentless psychology to our ordinary classifications in terms of beliefs, desires and intentions. Stich is not concerned to relate the two forms of description in any systematic way. He does not expect any neat isomorphism of individuation into either types or token of each mode of classification. His syntactic theory of mind is offered rather as a replacement for our everyday intentional discourse, not as a reduction, and thereby vindication of it. His theory does not, therefore, help us in our task, for it has been one of the assumptions of this book that intentional theory is so successful that it requires vindication rather than replacement. Moreover we were examining functionalism as a theory which reduced our intentional kinds, not one which eliminated them. Stich's theory, therefore, fails to provide us with what we need.

Not all functionalists who wish to offer a revision of the explanatory role of our intentional theory follow Stich's eliminative line. Some theorists adopt a *dual component* view of intentionality. (This view is also prompted by individualism – see Chapter Seven.) First, intentional descriptions make demands of the inner functional roles of an agent's physical states. This aspect of intentionality can be given an extensional functional explication. It is sufficient to individuate distinct intentional states (types) and characterise the conditional dependencies between them. It is on this component of our intentional descriptions that their explanatory role with regard to behaviour rests. Our intentional descriptions, however, also involve the assignment of truth conditions to beliefs, satisfaction conditions for desire, etc. That is, they involve the attribution to states of semantic content. According to dual component theorists this aspect of intentionality is independent of the first. Such theorists give different accounts of what they regard the determinants of semantic content to be. Some look to the causal origins of certain syntactic states in the world,[1] others to what states of affairs in the world such states are reliable indicators of;[2] yet others regard the attribution of semantic content as constrained by our overall interpretive theory of the organism, which is interest relative, and for many theorists indeterminate.[3] All such theorists agree, however, that the determinants of the semantic content of psychological states are irrelevant from the standpoint of the causal explanatory role of such states and are therefore incidental to the classification into psychological kinds. Thus Hartry Field:

> If the task of psychology is to state (i) the laws by which an organism's beliefs and desires evolve as he is subjected to sensory stimulations, and (ii) the laws by which these beliefs and desires affect his bodily movements; then semantic characterisations of beliefs and desires are irrelevant to psychology.[4]

The first component in a dual-component view of intentionality, therefore, requires the characterisation of a set of extensional dependencies between functionally characterised states, isomorphic with the dependencies between intentional ones. Such isomorphism is regarded as sufficient to justify a reduction of our intentional kinds to functional kinds. Aspects of their intentional descriptions not captured by such functional isomorphism are then viewed as incidental features of the way

[1] Harman 1977 and Devitt 1974.
[2] Field 1978 and Loar 1981.
[3] H. Putnam, 'Computational psychology and interpretation theory', in Putnam 1983.
[4] Field 1978.

such kinds are picked out, dependent for example on their being found in certain environmental conditions.

Such a suggestion, however, does not provide an exemption from the anti-reductionist arguments rehearsed in Chapter Four. There it was argued that our intentional descriptions are essential to the explanatory work of our intentional kinds. No reduction of these kinds is therefore possible which cannot capture this explanatory work. This argument is most easily accepted by those who see the explanatory work of our intentional kinds as *sui generis*. This, however, is not the case for the causal explanatory theorist. She has the option of accepting that there is distinctive non-causal explanatory work done by our intentional descriptions but, centrally, wants to argue that such descriptions yield a pattern of classification leading to empirical generalisations which support counterfactuals and conditionals. Her resistance to functionalist reduction must therefore be a resistance to the plausibility of finding functional characterisations of an extensional kind which will provide the isomorphism such dual-component theorists suggest. Any functional predicate which we devise must be projectible without the use of intentional considerations to all and only those actual and counterfactual cases to which our intentional characterisations lead us, and this is just what our previous arguments suggested was implausible.

One of the major difficulties facing any such syntactic theories is to give an account of computation, those patterns of relationships between intentional states which we characterise in terms of theoretical and practical reasoning. Hartry Field tries to do this by construing intentional states as extensionally characterised relations to sentence-analogues, which themselves are purely syntactic items. They are, however, items with an analogue of grammatical structure. Such sentence-analogues are items internal to the believer. Field's central suggestion is that we can capture the pattern of transformations which constitute both belief-based and desire-based reasoning in terms of patterns of causal relations between states whose sentence analogues bear certain relations to each other: these relations to be characterisable in a purely extensional way. For example, the fact that if we desire an end then *ceteris paribus* we desire the means to that end becomes:

> There is some connective → in the system of internal representation such that for all sentences S_1 and S_2 in the system whenever a person believes* 'S_1 → S_2' and desires* S_2 then he also desires* S_1.[1]

Not all functionalists who adopt a dual-component approach to content employ the assumption of an inner language of thought on which Field relies. In some of the writings of Brian Loar[2] certain states are individuated as perceptual beliefs by direct causal links to the environment, and as desires by functional links to bodily movements. Further non-perceptual beliefs are then individuated by conditional links to perceptual beliefs. Again, the patterns of transformation which constitute both belief-based and desire-based reasoning are specified by *listing* extensional conditional dependencies between such states. These dependencies are characterised by assigning syntactic structure to functional states but without the assumption that there are literal

[1] Ibid., 46.
[2] Loar 1981.

135

sentence analogues inside the head.[1] If we accept the arguments of the previous chapters then these lists must satisfy two conditions. They must be projectibly co-extensive with the patterns of intentional dependencies characterised within intentional theory, and they must be unified at the level of nomological extensional functional theory. Consider however McDowell, making a point concerning deductive rationality which extends, even more powerfully, to cases of inductive and practical reasoning:

> Deductive rationality is a capacity ... to hold beliefs when and because they follow deductively from other beliefs one holds ... this structure cannot be abstracted away

[1] One problem with the account is this. For both Field and Loar characterisation of the patterns of relations which are intended to capture reasoning depend on identifying states via the same syntactically characterised item. It is important for their theory that the same *type of item* recur within the characterisation of distinct beliefs* or desires* (for example, the terms S_1 and S_2 or the connective '$\rightarrow$' in the characterisation in the text). It is via the presence of such recurring items that patterns of reasoning are to be captured in what they hope is a purely formal way. They therefore need a criterion for identifying and re-identifying such syntactic items. Both theorists recognise the need and suggest that a functional criterion of type-identity will emerge in the course of developing our functional psychology. However, if we turn our attention to an analogy with computers, it is not clear that a criterion determining significant syntactic structure will necessarily emerge in a way that conforms to their reductive intentions. When we interpret a computer as 'reasoning', we interpret different tokens of syntactic items as representing the same proposition. In functionalist terminology we would be interpreting them as being of the *same syntactic type*. We may do this on the basis of a shared type or sound or position, and in many other ways. There is no mode of classification into syntactic types given by the physical make-up of the computer. We make the classification in the way that is useful to us. On what basis do we do it? Here is the problem. We make our classifications in a way that enables us to use the computer in our reasoning. We interpret items as syntactically the same if, on giving them the same *propositional content*, the transformations of the computer with regard to those

from relations between contents ... in such a way that we might hope to find the abstracted structure exemplified in the inter-relations among a system of items described in non-intentional terms ... someone who denied the claim would find it hard to explain how his position was consistent with the fact that there is no mechanical test for logical validity in general ... [1]

Such scepticism is linked to the deep unsatisfactoriness of an account of intentional explanation which separates off the semantic content of our intentional states from their explanatory role. For dual-component theorists our intentional descriptions serve to label states with certain extensional functional roles. They also serve some quite distinct purpose, which determines their content. These two aspects are quite independent. The functional role labelled by one content could equally well be captured by some other. Even Loar himself admits that the mutual independence of functional role and truth conditions is 'curious'.[2] In response it is difficult not to agree with McDowell:

> Consider how the idea applies to wants. What a want is a want for has nothing to do with the explanatory capacity of citing it. What then is the point of the notion of what a want is a want for? It lies in such facts as that when one gets what one wants, the wants cease to move one. This remarkable suggestion (for which see *Mind and Meaning*, 196-8) seems close to a reductio ad absurdum.[3]

The plausibility of the dual-component approach derives in part from the conception such theorists have of the explanatory goal of psychological theory. Field, for

items would yield true conclusions from true premises. In this way our classification into *syntactic kinds* is parasitic on our interpretation of the computer in *semantic* terms.

[1] McDowell 1985.
[2] Loar 1981, 194.
[3] McDowell 1985, 394n.

example, saw the task of psychology as stating 'the laws by which an organism's beliefs and desires evolve as he is subject to sensory stimulations and the laws by which these beliefs and desires affect his bodily movements'.[1] A psychology which had these goals would be quite different from the intentional theory we currently employ. Our intentional theory explains beliefs and desires as a response to environmental conditions characterised in terms of everyday concepts of micro- and macro-objects. Its output is intentional acts. Consequently it is often uncommitted regarding the bodily movements by which such acts are performed. These issues will receive discussion in the ensuing chapter, for the explanatory goal of psychology which Field envisages coincides with that of the individualist. Given the difference of the explanatory goals it is unsurprising that Field's psychology should fail to capture the explanatory work of our current intentional descriptions. We do not need to deny the possibility that a contentless psychology may emerge, linking extensional functional kinds to sensory imputs and bodily movement outputs. Indeed the functional kinds which such a psychology might develop may yield properties of key importance when considering what kinds of systems can form a supervenient base for intentional properties. It may be that systems satisfying Field and Loar's functional characterisation, when embedded within appropriate environments etc., may have intentional states. What is being denied is that such functional kinds and any generalisations in which they may be embedded can be regarded as *reducing* our current intentional kinds and explanatory theory.

[1] Field 1978.

4. Anti-reductionist materialism

If we reject the functionalist account of the mental, how are we to satisfy the requirements on a satisfactory theory of the mental, which initially appeared to provide its justification (see above, section 2)?

The intelligibility condition

We need to make a distinction between different kinds of intelligibility that can be required of the supervenience relation. If we accept supervenience claims for a set of properties then it is legitimate to ask for justification of such a belief. In the psychological case our reasons for accepting supervenience would be those supporting an overall materialist metaphysic; the need to provide a categorial grounding for our dispositional claims and for some people an acceptance of physicalism together with an acceptance of the principle that higher-level causal connections are mediated by causal connections at the physical level. We can also ask for justification of the belief that supervenience is *possible*, i.e. that it is possible for there to be physically sufficient conditions for intentional characterisations. To justify such a belief however does not require a reductive explication of our psychological descriptions, in a way which would enable us to derive them from physical descriptions. There are clearly cases where one description supervenes on another where no such derivation is possible. Take our ordinary descriptions of the world in terms of macro-objects such as tables and chairs. These supervene on descriptions in terms of our fundamental physical theories, but there is no reductive explication allowing us to derive one from the other. The intelligibility of the supervenience relation in this case comes from perceiving how our macro-object descriptions can be applied to a certain range of physical phenomena. An anti-reductionist can make the same claims of our intentional theory. The intelligibility of supervenience in this case, too, may well be provided only by showing how intentional descriptions can be applied to physical systems, rather than by providing a reductive account of such descriptions. This point can be made clearer by considering what kind of demarcation condition an anti-reductionist can provide (see below). One consequence of such a position is recognition that the law-like conditionals which are constitutive of the supervenience relation may not be the output of any systematic theory. They might rather be available only by inspecting the physical (and functional) characteristics of those systems which can be described intentionally.

The demarcation condition

Our psychological theory must make empirical demands of any system to which it applies. The challenge of the functionalist was that either we regard our theory as simply a useful device for systematising behaviour (instrumentalism) or it also makes demands of our inner states. If it does the latter, it is assumed that it is equivalent to reductive functionalism. This, however, is a mistake. In providing a demarcation condition the anti-reductionist can take over aspects of both the instrumentalist and the functionalist position, without adopting either. She can accept, with the functionalist, that our psychological descriptions make demands of a system's inner states, as well as behaviour in certain environments. She can accept with the instrumentalist that a system has psychological states if psychological descriptions can be successfully applied to it, without the need for a reductive explication of these descriptions.

We require of theories only that they make sense of the world, explain it and make fruitful predictions in their own terms. We do not demand that the mode of conceptualisation which each theory employs should necessarily be definable in terms external to the theory. Our intentional theory employs its own criteria for individuating and classifying the phenomena to which it applies. It provides a characterisation of our environment, our inner states and our behaviour. Such characterisations must make demands of the system. They must be teachable and projectible. There must be a distinction between a correct and incorrect application of them. But they need not be expressible in non-intentional vocabulary. In applying intentional descriptions to an agent we therefore seek a way of characterising the environment such that the agent can be attributed intentional states causally sensitive to environmental features thus characterised (for more on this see Chapter Seven). These environmental descriptions are couched not in the terms of fundamental physical theory (except when we are attributing thoughts about atoms, molecules, etc.) but in terms of our everyday concepts. These environmental descriptions supervene, without reduction, on descriptions in terms of physical theory. We look for a way of individuating the behaviour so that it is of a kind rationalised by the intentional states attributed to the system. The behavioural descriptions are couched in the terminology of intentional actions: waving, typing, writing letters, etc. These descriptions supervene without reduction on movements as characterised in terms of neuro-physiology. Both the environmental and behavioural descriptions are teachable and projectible. If we are faced with an agent who does not share our concepts, we have to learn *their* way of conceptualising their environment at the same time as constructing an intentional theory which applies to them. These points are well-worn, for they have been made many times by writers emphasising the interdependencies of our theory of translation for another language with our intentional theory for the speakers concerned.

If, however, the only anchorage of our intentional descriptions, the only facts to which they are answerable, were facts about the environment and behaviour, the intentional ascriptions which appear to refer to intervening variables between input and output would remain at the level of an *abstract* calculus. We could attribute to the system whatever set of states would be required to render intentional whatever behaviour is produced, and a range of alternatives might suit the behaviour equally well. This is the instrumentalist position. It is not, however, acceptable to the causal explanatory theorist. For such a theorist it is not the case that any attribution of intentional states will be equally legitimate, provided that it relates approximately to the system's actual behaviour. Distinct intentional descriptions which would perform that task will make different demands of the organisation of the agent's inner states. Our intentional descriptions can, therefore, be rendered true/false by the nature of these inner states and not just by actual behaviour. To attribute intentional states to a system is to attribute to it a wide range of dispositional properties, regarding how it will behave in certain circumstances. Such intentional actions will require a certain range of bodily movements, and the system's inner states must be such as would generate bodily movements which are susceptible to the appropriate descriptions in such circumstances. Moreover attribution of certain intentional descriptions requires conditional dependencies between a wide range of actual and potential behaviour which our physical states must be such as to make true. For example, if I have a desire to go to the cinema, induced by noticing an advertisement in the paper for a certain film, and this leads me to take a certain route into town at a certain time, and cancel arrangements to meet someone for a drink, then the complex set of physical states on which the description of my desire supervenes must be causally linked to input from the newspaper, must be causally involved in the production of the movements into town and the movements whereby I cancel my arrangements with my friend (and of course both these latter must be counterfactually interdependent). If my physical states did not intermesh in this way, intentional descriptions could not be successfully applied to me.

To go further in spelling out the demands of our intentional theory would require unpacking the whole theory. Enough has been said, however, to establish the following points. Our intentional descriptions make demands of the agent's behaviour, environment and inner physical states, demands which can be falsified if the theory is incorrectly applied. In spelling out these demands, however, the intentional theorist is not required to use non-intentional vocabulary. A theory can be empirical without being reducible. Its demarcation condition need not employ language from without the theory.

The need for explanatory vindication

We pointed out earlier in this chapter that the primary concern of functionalism was the ontological status of our intentional states rather than their explanatory role. Successful functionalist reduction would provide physical support for our intentional explanations only on a case-by-case basis, and this can be provided for equally by the relation of supervenience, in the absence of such reductive claims. The challenge to vindicate the projectibility of our intentional laws, provided by reductionists of a more classical kind, would not be aided by reduction of intentional generalisations to functional ones. We do not already have an accepted body of scientific theory, with its own nexus of generalisations whose kind classifications are extensional functional. Putative functional laws therefore would face the same challenge to vindicate their projectability as intentional ones. They, however, would lack the attendant body of theory and long history of successful use which provided an answer to the challenge at the intentional level. It is therefore clear that functionalist reduction is not required to vindicate our intentional explanations at either a particular or a general level, nor would it promote such an aim.

CHAPTER SEVEN

Postscript: Individualism and Intentional Explanation

1. Individualism vs. the world-dependence of thought

It has been the contention of this book that the explanatory role of intentional explanation is dependent on the intentional content of the states it invokes, and that such explanation is causal explanation. It has been suggested, moreover, that individuating conditions for intentional states, and thereby of intentional content, derive from the location of such states within a theory explaining the behaviour of intentional agents.

Such a view faces a challenge from a series of arguments developed in recent years about the determinants of content. The first component of such arguments concerns what I shall term *individualism*.[1] It is argued that, if the causal explanatory picture is correct, the psychological states invoked in explanations of behaviour must be individuated independently of the real relations in which they stand to actual object/kinds in the

---

[1] As used in Burge 1986b and Davies 1986. This thesis is sometimes referred to as methodological solipsism, but Fodor (1986) used that term to imply the need for explanatory constructs which are syntactic not semantic, which is (initially) an independent claim. Fodor also uses the term individualism, but allows within it some taxonomies in terms of relational properties which my usage would exclude.

environment of their owners. In its materialist form, with which I shall be primarily concerned, such a requirement is equated with narrow supervenience, an agent's explanatory psychological states must supervene only on internal states of their body. The second component concerns *the world-dependence of thought*. Much recent work[1] has been concerned to display that the content of the attitudes we presently attribute to intentional agents is conditioned by their environment and/or social community. It is therefore dependent on states of affairs outside them and flouts the requirement of narrow supervenience.

In the light of these two sets of arguments there has developed an orthodoxy about the alternatives open. Those who wish to maintain a causal explanatory view of the psychological accept the need to construct *a revised content* for explanatory purposes, which respects narrow supervenience.[2] Those who are impressed by the role which our present world-dependent content plays in explanation regard the motivations for such revisions as misplaced attempts to fit intentional explanation into a scientific model.[3] They hold on to unrevised intentional content, but reject its role in causal explanation. What appears to be accepted by both sides is an assumption that a world-dependent content could not be fitted into causal explanation.

2. Arguments for individualism

(i) Stephen Stich has argued for individualism by claiming that the behaviour we devise our psychological

---

[1] E.g. Putnam, 'The Meaning of Meaning', in Putnam 1975. Burge 1979, 1982, 1986a & b.

[2] E.g. Fodor 1980, 1985, 1986; Loar 1981, 1982; McGinn 1982.

[3] See articles by Pettit, McCulloch and McDowell in McDowell & Pettit 1986.

theory to explain is behaviour which would be common to
an agent and her doppelgänger (an atom-by-atom
replica). This Stich calls his replacement argument:

> suppose ... that while ... asleep I am kidnapped and
> replaced by the replica. It would appear that if the crime
> were properly concealed, no one (apart from the
> kidnappers and myself) would be the wiser. For the
> replica ... would behave just as I would in all
> circumstances   since psychology is the science which
> aspires to explain behaviour, any states or processes or
> properties which are not shared by Stich and his
> identically behaving replica must surely be irrelevant to
> psychology.[1]

Stich recognises that there are descriptions of the
agent's behaviour which would not be applicable to his
replica, e.g. the replica could not sell the car he finds
himself with, for he did not own it. Such descriptions
however will not, he claims, feature in the taxonomy of
behaviour which a scientific psychology could construct
causal generalisations to explain.

(ii) In Chapter Two it was argued that when we act
intentionally our explanatory intentional states are
necessary in each case not only for the performance of a
given intentional act, but for the occurrence of the bodily
movements such acts require. If I did not intend to write
I would not be moving my fingers in certain ways. In
Chapter Five the assumptions of explanatory physicalism were accepted. Sufficient conditions can be found in
physical terms for behaviour characterised physically. To
maintain these two claims together such physically
sufficient conditions must be sufficient for the necessary
intentional states in each case. If physical conditions
sufficient for a bodily movement can be provided by

[1] Stich 1983, 165.

internal physical states of the agent, then these claims appear to provide support for narrow supervenience.

(iii) Jerry Fodor argues that for explanatory purposes we need to classify together states with the same causal powers. If we accept that psychological kinds can vary with variations in environment and the agent's relations to that environment, without differences in their internal physical states, we would be assuming that the causal powers of our psychological states could alter without alterations in our physiological states. But there is no mechanism by which this can be done: 'You can't affect the causal powers of a person's mental states without affecting his physiology (that's not a conceptual claim or a metaphysical claim: it's a contingent fact about how God made the world).'[1]

Behind each of these arguments for individualism is an assumption that environmental determinants of content which are not reflected in differences in internal physical states are causally inert in respect of behaviour. Our explanatory psychological taxonomy should therefore exclude them.

3. The world-dependence of thought

The psychological facts which we currently invoke in intentional explanations of behaviour do not respect individualist constraints. Instead features/objects of an agent's environment, and the agent's relations to such features, are invoked as determinants of the contents which we attribute to intentional states; contents which could not be attributed were those objects/features to be different. In short the thoughts we deal in are world-dependent.

[1] Fodor 1986, 248.

7. Postscript

The first set of examples is the least controversial. When we attribute states of knowing, perceiving or remembering to an agent we are committed to the truth of what is known, the existence of what is perceived, and the past occurrence of what is remembered. All these clearly make demands of states of affairs outside of the agent's head, and of the agent's relations to such states of affairs. We do moreover utilise such intentional states in our explanations of behaviour, e.g.: *Q*. How did you get here so quickly? *A*. I remembered the way. *Q*. Why did you go to that house? *A*. I knew the headmaster lived there. *Q*. Why did you swerve? *A*. I saw the cat in the road.

A second set of examples is also familiar and concerns what have been termed *de re* attitudes. Such attitudes are those whose correct attribution requires the existence of some object (or kind) other than the agent and some other than semantic relation between the agent and that object or kind. *De re* attitudes are commonly ascribed using demonstratives or proper names, although we can use definite descriptions in a way that carries such commitments. Again such attitudes are used in intentional explanations of behaviour, e.g.: 'That is the bangle he most liked, which is why he chose it.' 'The Headmaster is the one she is angry with, which is why she won't invite him.' 'She thinks Angela Davies' classes the most interesting, which is why she attends them.' The inclusion of such *de re* attitudes in our intentional explanations appears an essential component if we are to explain particular actions. Thus Jennifer Hornsby:

> If your belief that it is going to rain is to lead you to take your umbrella, then you need (for example) to want not to get wet and to believe that umbrellas keep the rain off, and to have no other countervailing desires or interfering beliefs. But equally certainly, if your belief that it is going to rain is to lead you to take your umbrella, then you need

to believe of something that is your umbrella, that it is your umbrella.[1]

Without such a *de re* belief the other intentional states do not appear sufficient to explain the umbrella taking.

Recent work has shown the world-dependence of thoughts traditionally regarded as *de dicto*. Thoughts that had been regarded as characterising the world from the agent's point of view none the less depend for their individuation on features of the agent's environment. Tyler Burge and Hilary Putnam,[2] among others, have given examples of our characterisation of an agent's thoughts being dependent on what kinds in their world they are in relation to, and their membership of a linguistic community which relates to these kinds in certain ways. These kinds/linguistic practices may differ without such differences being reflected in the internal physical states of the agent. Best known of these examples is Putnam's example of Twin Earth,[3] where my doppelgänger interacts with a substance which appears to her as water does to me. However, it has the chemical structure XYZ and not H_2O. Her thoughts, despite her atom-by-atom duplication of me, would be thoughts not about water, but about, let's say, '(t)water'. According to Putnam, then, someone meaning what they do by a natural-kind word 'is determined by a scientifically ascertainable fact about the world they live in'.[4] Burge's examples have shown that the failure of narrow supervenience which this entails is not confined to natural-kind terms, but can work for any cases where there is an element of shared division of linguistic labour.

[1] Hornsby 1986, 101.
[2] See p. 146, n. 1.
[3] Putnam, 'The Meaning of Meaning', op. cit.
[4] McDowell & Pettit 1986, 1.

7. Postscript

Imagine someone who believes she has arthritis in the thigh. She knows many general facts about arthritis, but is ignorant of the fact that it cannot occur outside joints. We could none the less attribute such thoughts concerning arthritis to her. Now imagine a counterfactual world in which there is no difference in what is in the subject's head, but 'arthritis' is used for any rheumatoid ailment. In that world the subject's thoughts cannot be characterised as thoughts about arthritis.[1]

What these sets of examples challenge is 'a conception of psychological facts as facts about individuals which hold independently of their relation to the external world'.[2]

4. Some revisionist proposals

The individualist's response to these considerations is a revisionist one. It consists of decomposing our intentional explanations into two components, one component of which satisfies the demands of an individualistic psychology and the other which simply attaches to that some facts about the individual's world. The psychological element in our intentional explanations is then regarded as confined to the first component. Such a suggestion seems very familiar in the light of our previous discussion of functionalism. The connection is not accidental. Most causal explanatory theorists are functionalists, and if they also accept individualist

[1] Burge 1979.
[2] McDowell & Pettit 1986, 6. Nor are such world-dependent psychological facts confined to our everyday intentional explanations. For example, both learning theory and psycho-linguistics employ a taxonomy based on relations between agents and items outside the head. See Kitcher 1985.

demands they have a double motivation for a revisionary account of intentional content. In its present form it resists both functionalist and individualist constraints. Ideally then, for such theorists, adopting a dual-component approach will isolate from our intentional descriptions a purely psychological component which will be susceptible to functionalist explication and respect narrow supervenience. Recognition of this double motivation should not blind us to the distinct nature of the two sets of constraints. Functionalism is aiming for explication in order to render materialism intelligible. The functionalist explications are required to capture what it really is to be in a certain kind of intentional state and provide for the explanatory work of our intentional descriptions without use of intentional vocabulary. In terms of its own project it is not required to confine itself to states inside the agent's body and could include functional relations to items in the agent's environment.[1] Our arguments against functionalism rested on scepticism concerning the possibility of capturing extensionally a network of conditional dependencies isomorphic with our intentional ones; and, inter-connectedly, on a recognition of the need for intentional vocabulary to capture the explanatory work of our psychological states. These arguments do not necessarily render all dual-component views unsatisfactory. The individualist project requires that the internal physical states of an agent form a supervenient base sufficient for the attribution of psychological states which perform the explanatory role of our current intentional descriptions. Individualists do not have to accept functionalist reduction. Our arguments against such reduction therefore need not exclude all dual-component theories.

[1] See, e.g., Harman 1982.

7. Postscript

Our anti-functionalist arguments have, however, provided us with a condition of adequacy for any such theories. If the revised states are to play the explanatory role of our current intentional states, the 'inner component' must possess intentional, that is representational, content which is linked in rationalising ways to characterisations of the agent's environment and behaviour. If such content is lacking, such theories would simply be offering a non-psychological characterisation of part of the supervenient base of our intentional descriptions, and this is quite a different project. What this condition of adequacy rules out is dual-component theories of the kind suggested by Field or Loar.[1] While these can satisfy individualist demands, they do so at the cost of separating out the explanatory work of psychology from considerations of semantic content. As such they simply change the subject of explication.

At first sight is may look as if revisionist accounts satisfying this condition of adequacy can be provided:

> The strategy is to argue that within each non-internal psychological state that enters into the explanation of some action or behaviour we can locate an 'internal core state' which can assume the causal-explanatory role of the non-internal state; we would in fact argue that this internal core is the causal and explanatory core of the non-internal state.[2]

In terms of our first set of examples it might be suggested that we decompose the explanations so that their genuinely explanatory components deal in beliefs rather than knowledge, seemings instead of perceptions and apparent memories. In the case of *de re* beliefs it is claimed that we could withdraw from the *de re* mode and

[1] Field 1978 and Loar 1981, 1982. See above, Chapter Six.
[2] Kim 1982, 65.

153

substitute a characterisation of the agent's states which avoids such existential commitment. For example, a demonstrative thought, 'that is pretty', might decompose into: (i) 'Whatever stands in φ relation to me is pretty' (the psychological component), and (ii) A certain object standing in a φ relation to me (the contribution of the world). The psychological component could then remain stable and explain the agent's behaviour,[1] whether or not the world made its contribution. The Twin Earth cases present more problems, for we do not have currently available an expressible content which we could attribute to the thought of both me and my doppelgänger. But for many revisionists it is assumed that such a characterisation could be devised, via the construction of a new language respecting individualist constraints.

At each point along this series of revisionist proposals objections are forthcoming, objections that the revised content we are allowed does not do the explanatory work that we require. If I want to explain my avoiding hitting the cat, it seems important that I saw her and did not just take myself to. The loss of *de re* attitudes seems to carry a corresponding loss of an ability intentionally to explain action on particular objects. This can be shown most clearly with demonstrative thoughts. If I intend to take the pills which the doctor prescribes, such an intention will not adequately explain my taking certain pills, even if they are what the doctor prescribed, unless I believe, of these pills, that they are.[2] Such intentional

---

[1] See Blackburn 1984, 9 and Searle 1983. It is not a sufficient argument against such views that the descriptive decompositions which they favour would not be articulable by the agents concerned.

[2] Peacocke 1981. Lynne Rudder Baker 1982, however, challenges the claim that perceptual demonstrative beliefs can play a genuine explanatory role with regard to intentional acts on particular objects. Baker's examples concern an agent who is attributed perceptual demonstrative beliefs, consequent on distinct sensory modes of

action on particular objects seems distinct from cases where all that can be characterised intentionally is our taking ourselves to be performing an action of a certain kind, and the world providing an object in our way. Imagine two distinct cases of my picking up a duster[1] which is in front of me. In the first case I pick up the duster I have seen, touched, etc. The duster is causally responsible for certain inner states of mine, which are then responsible for the movements I make, which result in my successfully picking it up. When these (and some other) conditions are satisfied we would attribute demonstrative thoughts to me concerning the duster, including an intention to pick up that one. Such an intention then explains my intentional action of picking up just that duster. In a contrasting case I have been subject to a series of hallucinations, whereby it seems to me that there is a duster in front of me, etc. These lead to me reaching out and grabbing and, fortuitously, there is a duster there which I pick up. We could arrange our example so that the inner physical states of each agent are the same in each case and there is a set of *de dicto* beliefs which are common to both occasions. In individualist terms such beliefs explain intentionally the behaviour which is common to both (reaching out and grasping). The successful picking up of a duster is then explained by the world co-operating and placing a duster in their grasp. Such an account, however, seems to miss a crucial distinction between the two cases. In the first case

---

interaction, about each of two objects in front of her, that *it* is the most valuable. But, wanting to pick up the most valuable object, the agent picks only one. Baker, however, does not establish that the attitudes which the agent has to each object are the same at the moment of choice. When choosing it appears that she has a demonstrative thought 'that is the most valuable' only of the object chosen.

[1] I am indebted to Paul Gilbert for this example; for further discussion see Gilbert 1987.

the agent intentionally picked up a particular duster, an act explained by a demonstrative intention to do just that. In the second case no such intentional act or demonstrative intention could be attributed to her. The agent may say, 'I intend to pick up that duster', but does not thereby succeed in expressing a demonstrative thought. Indeed, on becoming aware of the hallucination, she herself would no longer attempt to characterise her intention in this way. Moreover in the second case, although her reaching and grasping was intentional, it is not possible to construe her picking up the particular duster she did as an intentional act. It therefore appears that there is an intentional act and an explanation in terms of intentional states available in the first case, but not the second, contrary to individualist assumptions. Parallel examples could be constructed for other cases of *de re* thoughts involved in actions explanations.

Such objections arise even where we accept that the revisionist project is a possible one; that is, where we assume that it is possible for states which respect narrow supervenience to be attributed intentional content. But this possibility is itself intensely problematic. The distinguishing feature of the intentionality of psychological states is that states of an agent are individuated by means of sentences whose meanings are fixed by their representational role with regard to states of affairs in the world. The key question which has to be confronted by any theory of intentional content is what is it that determines that our intentional states have the content they do? This is a question which concerns our beliefs as much as the things we know; the content of our apparent memories, as well as our veridical ones; how things seem to us to be, as well as how we successfully perceive them to be; descriptive thoughts as well as demonstrative ones.

156

7. Postscript

There is an example of Putnam's[1] in which he discussed an ant crossing and criss-crossing its tracks in the sand until the result looks like an accurate caricature of Winston Churchill. We would be most disinclined to claim that this was a representation of Winston Churchill, for neither the ant, nor the series of lines it creates, have any connection at all with the man. The likeness is a pure accident. What is lacking, of course, is an intention on the part of the ant to create a likeness of Winston Churchill. But this only pushes the question back a stage, for we still need an account of what gives the intention such a content. No purely intrinsic features of a state 'whether of material stuff, mind stuff, or soul stuff' can guarantee a representational content *per se*. The world-dependent theorist very plausibly suggests that the more that is required consists in appropriate connections between such states and objects/properties in the world. It is, of course, a major task to characterise what these appropriate connections are; but for such a theorist they are real relations between agents and some actual existent objects and property instances in their environment. Tyler Burge makes the point when discussing why we are unwilling to attribute understanding to machines. What is wrong with machines so far, Burge claims, is that they do nothing to indicate that 'their symbols have any semantic, extra-linguistic significance; and for this to be shown the machines must recognise and initiate correlations between symbols and what they symbolise. The contents of their thoughts would be determined by what actual features of reality they correlated their symbols with.'[2]

Such arguments present a challenge to the individualist, for if the content of thought is not determined by the

[1] Putnam 1981, ch. 1.
[2] Burge 1977.

objects/features of the world the agent interacts with, what does determine it, and determine it in such a way that the world seems to the agent to have such objects and features? Each of the revisionist responses to world-dependent characterisation of thought, yielded thoughts which represented the world as being a certain way to the agent; for the whole character of intentional explanation rests on such representational features. The key issue is what determines that our thoughts have the representational features they do? Peacocke puts the point as follows:

> One might be tempted to say that the inward looking theorist is achieving only an account of the content. 'It is from the inside as if it were the case that *p*', rather than the content that *p* itself. But even this is too strong: for the content 'It is from the inside as if it were the case that *p*' embeds the content that *p*, and the inward-looking theorist does not have an account even of this unless he has an account of the embedded content that *p*.[1]

To focus the question in this way is not to deny the fact, often reiterated by individualists,[2] that our intentional states are fallible. Things can seem to us to be ways which they are not. Clearly any account of content formation must respect such fallibility. That itself, however, does not justify an assumption that how things seem to an agent is something which can be fixed quite independently of the world and their relation to it.[3] When we reach that point we seem to have no resource other than to assume that inner states gain representational content 'by magic'.[4]

[1] Peacocke 1986, ch. 4.
[2] See McGinn 1982.
[3] Burge 1986a.
[4] See John McDowell, 'Singular thought and inner space' in McDowell & Pettit 1986.

7. Postscript

The challenge presented by these considerations seems insufficiently recognised by theorists such as Loar, who simply assert that on the basis of the internal causal roles of the agent's physical states alone (that is, the pattern of stimulation of the agent's sensory nerves, the internal counterfactual relations between states, and their links to bodily movements) we can attribute content to their thoughts of a recognisably representational kind (which none the less lacks objective reference and truth conditions):

> The individualistic conceptual roles of a person's thoughts would account for − as it is completely natural to say − how the person represents the world to himself. That seems like some kind of content.[1]

Fodor[2] makes some attempt to recognise the challenge. He accepts a dual-component account of intentionality and links the two components by arguing that 'narrow content' plus context determines truth conditions. It is however truth-conditional content which we use in the characterisations of such states and consequently the dimension of content which I share with my doppelgänger may not be independently expressible. Philip Pettit has a shot at expressing it. The narrow content is captured in terms of what the broad content would be, were the 'world willing'. The narrow content of 'A wants this cup' becomes 'A is such that, given a world in which this cup exists, he wants this cup'.[3] What remains unclear is why the fact that we can individuate a state by the fact that, *in this world*, it yields a desire for a particular cup, should establish that it has content of a

[1] Loar 1985.
[2] Fodor 1986.
[3] Philip Pettit, 'Broad-minded explanation and psychology' in McDowell & Pettit 1986, 32.

159

representational kind, independent of such relational features. This problem is particularly acute once we recognise that the world may be willing in many different ways, and the same pattern of internal functional dependencies mediate different environments.

5. Challenging the individualist's motivation

The considerations of the previous section should make us sceptical of the possibility of accommodating our intentional theory to the constraints of individualism. We therefore need to scrutinise more carefully the arguments which provided the motivation for the attempt.

Both Stich and Fodor assume that the behaviour which is the proper explanatory concern of psychological theory is behaviour which an agent and her doppelgänger share. They therefore take the appropriate output of psychological theory to be behaviour individuated in terms of bodily movements. This is a reflection of their functionalist, as well as their individualist, concerns. However, the intentional acts for which we seek explanation are not individuated in this way. Frequently what we are seeking to explain is an agent's interaction with some part of her environment, picking up a cup, tracking down a lost aunt, or making dandelion wine. If the output of our intentional theory is classified in such a world-dependent way, it should be no surprise that a taxonomy of states designed to explain such acts should also reflect, not just inner states of an agent, but their relations to their world.

It would, of course, be open to an individualist to argue for a revision of the explananda of our intentional theory to correspond to the revision of the explanans. What is explained psychologically is only the bodily movements, the rest comes from the world. So Kim claims:

> the action of turning on the burner, insofar as this is
> thought to involve the burner going on, is not an action
> that it is the proper business of psychological theory to
> explain or predict. The job of psychological explanation is
> done once it has explained the bodily action of turning a
> knob.[1]

Indeed strictly for Kim all that could be explained
psychologically would be the bodily movements involved
in turning. But such restrictions face difficulties.
Intentional explanation requires a matching between the
content of my intention and the content of my action, and
this will not always be found for actions characterised as
bodily movements. Moreover, even where I move my
fingers intentionally, that is not all I do intentionally. I
also intentionally tie my shoelaces or turn on the burner,
intentional acts missing from the revisionist picture. All
cases of genuine psychological explanation become
analogous to the second case of grasping a duster,
discussed above: namely, cases where I intentionally
grasp, and the world fortuitously places, a duster in my
hand.

If we start with individualism with regard to the
explananda of psychology we shall be motivated towards
individualism with regard to the explanans. But what
would provide the argument for the initial restriction?
One line of thought might be that, to explain my turning
on the burner, more is required than the agent's
intentional states: the world has to contain a burner to be
turned on. We therefore need to look at some alternative
characterisation of the behaviour if we wish for what is
explained purely psychologically. If we accepted such

---

[1] Kim 1982, 64; see also Hornsby 1986.

reasoning, however, we would need to revise our conception of what psychological states explain even more radically than individualists suggest. Even bodily movements require the working of nerves and muscles in my body which have no psychological features, and so such movements are not explained purely by psychological states. If the existence of such items can be presupposed without requiring us to reject our intentional explanations of acts construed as bodily movements, why must the need for the world to contain a burner, for us to switch it on, exclude such switchings from the domain of intentional activity?[1]

If we reject the individualist constraint on the output of psychological theory, we can regard the task of intentional explanation as being an agent's successful negotiation of her environment. On this view to attribute intentionality presupposes a degree of adaptation which enables an agent to gain knowledge of properties and particulars of her world, in the light of which she can respond discriminately to satisfy her wants. It is only when there is a degree of success that we have the basis to invoke intentional explanation. On such a view our paradigm of intentional explanation would be that given for intentionally picking up a particular duster in the first case discussed above. Were *all* cases of the second kind, where a duster was only fortuitously present, we would have no basis for attributing intentionality. Within such a model there is no requirement that our intentional theory should always characterise my behaviour and that of my doppelgänger as being of the same kind, for our common bodily movements mediate interaction with distinct environments.

Writers who accept these points have often interpreted

[1] See Hornsby 1986.

162

them as support for a non-causal view of intentional theory. The job of causal explanation, it is assumed, is best done by an explanans and explanandum which conforms to individualist constraints, whether or not the explanans can be regarded as content-involving or the explanandum as intentional. The explanatory work of states with broad content is distinct; normalising rather than regularising.[1] What remains unclear is the reason for restricting causal explanations in this way. It seems uncontroversial to assume that each time we act intentionally some bodily movements occur which are causally explicable by internal physical states of the agents. Still open for debate is a suggestion that supervenient on such inner states and bodily movements arises a taxonomy of states in terms of functional or 'narrow psychological' characteristics which generates a body of causal generalisations. However, even if this latter possibility is accepted, there is no reason why it should constitute our favoured causal theory with regard to behaviour. The existence of neither of these individualist theories would give us reason to reject the possibility of a set of causal regularities in which the taxonomies employed are broad rather than narrow.

To defend this possibility we need to look again at the arguments for individualism concerning causal powers and over-determination. We shall start with Fodor's arguments from causal powers. If we characterise the output of our psychological theory in a world-dependent way, what our psychological states enable us to do will be different, e.g. on earth and Twin Earth. My utterance 'Bring water' will result in H_2O being brought here, and XYZ on Twin Earth. Fodor considers this kind of response to his argument, and rejects it. 'Identity of

[1] See both McDowell, op. cit. and Pettit, op. cit., in McDowell & Pettit 1986.

causal powers has to be assessed ACROSS contexts, not WITHIN contexts,'[1] he claims. My states and my doppelgänger's states would have the same consequences if we were both on earth, or both on Twin Earth. Therefore they must be classified as the same kind. However, as pointed out by Martin Davies,[2] such a claim regarding taxonomy is not obviously compatible with Fodor's acceptance that some relational properties, e.g. 'being a planet' can be reflected in our kind classifications. A chunk of matter physically similar to a planet would behave like a planet, if suitably placed, but we do not classify it as a planet until it is so placed. Some sciences are tied to a certain 'range of actual and possible contexts, they – and the taxonomy they deploy – presume upon certain environmental factors not being varied'.[3] If the task of intentional theory is that outlined above, we would expect our intentional taxonomy to be tied in exactly this way.[4]

How are we to accommodate the individualist argument which derived from the fact that in most cases we would not move our bodies the way we do, when acting intentionally, if we lacked the explanatory intentional states we have? This fact, when combined

[1] Fodor 1986.

[2] Davies 1986.

[3] Davies 1986, 270-1.

[4] But surely if the chemical constitution of water changes, without the alteration being brought to our attention, our thoughts do not thereby change? Surely we still intend to drink glasses of water? This may be right. The content of our thoughts is fixed by our location in a given world and environment and requires consideration of the causal origins of our dispositions in that world. Once content is fixed, mere variation in our circumstances need not change it. If I am suddenly transposed to Twin Earth my thoughts may still concern water. But this does not undermine the claim that, had I been placed on Twin Earth initially, the content of my thoughts would have been different while my physical constitution remained the same.

with explanatory physicalism, led to the requirement that an agent's inner physical states provide sufficient conditions for her intentional states. Such claims, however, are anchored in a specific set of conditions. It is in just the circumstances which prevailed that, had I not wanted to make a telephone call, I would not have moved my hand in the way required to lift the receiver. In considering the counter-factual possibility the circumstances are held stable, and these include the general and particular items in the agent's environment, her relations to them and the laws of working of her world. It is only, given all this, that her inner physical states are sufficient for her intentional states. There is a further point. The sufficiency of a set of physical states for certain intentional states does not exclude the possibility of other necessary conditions for those intentional states, provided these further conditions are also necessary for the inner physical states. The necessity of states outside the agent for the occurrence of certain bodily movements has been resisted by the thought that were the agent replaced by an atom-by-atom replica the same kind of bodily movements would occur. But this is to handle counterfactual possibilities the wrong way. In a given world (without such a replica) the presence of certain patterns of physical dispositions will be a consequence of the agent's interaction with her world and environment. In the circumstances in which we find ourselves it is perfectly plausible to assume that, had certain objects/kinds in our environment been absent, our inner physical states and corresponding dispositions would be different from what they are. We have no reason to suppose that the environmental conditions on which the representational features of our intentional states partly supervene are causally inert with regard to our intentional acts or the bodily movements which they require.

6. Conclusion

The object of this chapter has been to resist the constraints which the individualist attempts to impose on our intentional theory. If we regard the explanatory goal, within which our intentional taxonomy is deployed, as explaining agents' successful and well-adapted inter-actions with their actual environments, the motivations for such an individualist position are undermined. The content of thought which we attribute within such a theory reflects the agent/world interaction which is its explanatory goal, and our attribution of intentionality to ourselves and others goes hand in hand with our characterisation of the environment of those to whom we attribute it.

Bibliography

Armstrong, D.H. (1968) *A Materialist Theory of Mind*, London: Routledge

Baker, Lynne Rudder (1982) *'De re* belief in action', *Philosophical Review*

Barwell, I. & Lennon, K. (1982/3) 'The principle of sufficient reason', *Proceedings of the Aristotelian Society*

Blackburn, S. (1984) *Spreading the Word*, Oxford: OUP

—— (1986) 'Finding psychology', *Philosophical Quarterly*

Block, N. (ed.) (1980) *Readings in Philosophy of Psychology* vols. 1 and 2, Cambridge, Mass: Harvard UP

Boyd, R. (1979) 'Metaphor and theory change', in Ortony (ed.) 1979

—— (1982) 'On the current status of scientific realism', *Erkenntnis* 17

—— (1984a) 'Natural kinds, homoeostasis and the limits of essentialism', Manuscript

—— (1984b) 'Materialism without reductionism', Manuscript

Bratman, M. (1979) 'Practical reasoning and weakness of the will', *Nous* 13

—— (1984) 'Two faces of intention', *Philosophical Review* 93

—— (1985) 'Davidson's theory of intention', in Vermazen & Hintikka 1985

Burge, T. (1977) 'Belief in de re', *Journal of Philosophy*

—— (1979) 'Individualism and the mental', in French et al. 1979

—— (1982) 'Other bodies', in Woodfield 1982

—— (1986a) 'Cartesian error and perception', in McDowell & Pettit 1986

(1986b) 'Individualism and psychology', *Philosophical Review* 95

Cartwright, N. (1983) *How the Laws of Physics Lie*, Oxford: OUP

Charles, D. (1982/3) 'Rationality and irrationality', *Proceedings of the Aristotelian Society*

—— (1984a) *Aristotle's Philosophy of Action*, London: Duckworth

—— (1984b) 'World dependent thoughts', Manuscript

—— (1984c) 'Intention, practical reason and acrasia', Manuscript

—— (1985a) 'Paradox lost and paradox regained', Manuscript

—— (1985b) 'Aristotle on materialism and the explanation of behaviour', *Princeton Colloquium*

Churchland, Patricia Smith (1980) 'A perspective on mind-brain

Bibliography

research', *Journal of Philosophy* 77

Churchland, Paul (1981) 'Eliminative materialism and propositional attitudes', *Journal of Philosophy* 78

—— (1984) *Matter and Consciousness*, Cambridge MA: MIT/Bradford Books

Cummins, R. (1983) *The Nature of Psychological Explanation*, Cambridge, Mass: MIT Press

Currie, G. & Musgrove, A. (1985), *Popper and the Human Sciences*, Dordrecht: Nijhoff

Dancy, J. (1981) 'Moral Properties', *Mind* 90

Davidson, D. (1980) *Essays on Actions and Events*, Oxford: OUP

—— (1984) *Inquiries into Truth and Interpretation*, Oxford: OUP

Davies, M. (1981) *Meaning, Quantification and Necessity*, London: Routledge

—— (1983) 'Function in perception', *Australasian Journal of Philosophy*

—— (1986) 'Externality, psychological explanation and narrow content', *Proceedings of the Aristotelian Society Supplementary Volume*

Dennett, D. (1979) *Brainstorms*, Brighton: Harvester

—— (1987) *The Intentional Stance*, Cambridge, Mass: MIT Press

Devitt, M. (1974) 'Singular terms', *Journal of Philosophy* 71

Dretske, F. (1988) *Explaining Behaviour*, Cambridge Mass: MIT Press

Evans, G. (1981) 'Reply to Wright', in Holtzmann and Leich 1981

—— (1982) *Varieties of Reference*, Oxford: OUP

Feigl, Maxwell & Scriven (1958) *Minnesota Studies in the Philosophy of Science*, Vol. 2, Minneapolis: University of Minnesota

Field, H. (1975) 'Conventionalism and instrumentalism in semantics', *Nous* 9

—— (1977) 'Logic, meaning and conceptual role', *Journal of Philosophy* 74

—— (1978) 'Mental representation', *Erkenntnis* 13

Fodor, K. (1975) *The Language of Thought*, Brighton: Harvester

—— (1980) 'Methodological solipsism considered as a research strategy in cognitive psychology', *Behavioural and Brain Sciences* 3

—— (1981) *Representations*, Brighton: Harvester

—— (1985) 'Narrow content', Manuscript

—— (1986) 'Individualism and supervenience', *Proceedings of the Aristotelian Society Supplementary Volume*

Frege, G. (1960) 'Sense and reference', in Geach & Black 1960

French et al. (edd.) (1979) *Midwest Studies in Philosophy*, Vol. 4, Minneapolis: University of Minnesota Press

Geach, P. and Black, M. (edd.) (1960) *Frege: Philisophical Writings*, Blackwell

Gilbert, P. (1985) 'Acquaintance and belief de re', Manuscript

Goldman, A. (1970) *A Theory of Human Action*, Prentice-Hall

Bibliography

Grice, H.P. (1971) 'Intention and uncertainty', *Proceedings of the British Academy* 57

—— (1975) 'Method in philosophical psychology (from the banal to the bizarre)', *Proceedings and Addresses of the American Philosophical Association* 48

Grice, H.P. & Baker, J. (1985) 'Davidson on weakness of will', in Vermazen & Hintikka 1985

Harman, G. (1977) 'How to use propositions', *American Philosophical Quarterly* 14

—— (1982) 'Conceptual role semantics', *Notre Dame Journal of Formal Logic* 23

Haugeland, J, (1982) 'Weak supervenience', *American Philosophical Quarterly* 19

Healey, R. (ed.) (1981) *Reduction, Time and Identity*, Cambridge: CUP

Hellman, G. & Thompson, F. (1975) 'Physicalism: Ontology, Determination & Reduction', *Journal of Philosophy* 72

Hempel, C. (1965) *Aspects of Scientific Explanation*, New York: The Free Press

Holtzman, L. & Leich, S. (edd.) (1981) *Wittgenstein: to follow a rule*, London: Routledge

Honderich, T. (1981) 'Psycho-physical law-like connections and their problems', *Inquiry* 24

Hopkins, J. & Wollheim, R. (1982) *Philosophical Essays on Freud*, Cambridge: CUP

Hornsby, J. (1980/1981) 'Which physical events are mental events?', *Proceedings of the Aristotelian Society*

—— (1986) 'Physicalist thinking and behaviour' in McDowell & Pettit 1986

Hurley, S. (1985/6) 'Conflict, akrasia and cognitivism', *Proceedings of the Aristotelian Society*

Jackson, F. (1980) 'Ontological commitment and paraphrase', *Philosophy* 55

Kim, J. (1973) 'Causes and counterfactuals', *Journal of Philosophy* 70

—— (1978) 'Supervenience and nomological incommensurables', *American Philosophical Quarterly* 41

—— (1984) 'Self understanding and rationalising explanations', *Philosophia Naturalis* 21

—— (1984/5) 'Concepts of supervenience', *Philosophy and Phenomenological Research* 45

—— (1985) 'Psychophysical laws' in LePore & McLaughlin 1985

Kitcher, P. (1985) 'Narrow taxonomy and wide functionalism', *Philosophy of Science* 52

Klagge, J. (1988) 'Supervenience, ontological and ascriptive', *Australasian Journal of Philosophy* 66, no. 4

Kripke, S. (1979) 'A puzzle about belief', in Margalit 1979

169

Bibliography

—— (1980) *Naming and Necessity*, Oxford: Blackwell

Lakatos, I. (ed.) (1970) *Criticism and the Growth of Knowledge*, Cambridge: CUP

Lennon, K. (1984) 'Anti-reductionist materialism', *Inquiry* 27

LePore, E. & McLaughlin, B. (1985) *Actions and Events: Perspectives on the Philosophy of Donald Davidson*, Oxford: Blackwell

Lewis, D. (1973) *Counterfactuals*, Oxford: Blackwell

—— (1983) *Philosophical Papers*, vol. 1, Oxford: OUP

Loar, B. (1981) *Mind and Meaning*, Cambridge: CUP

—— (1982) 'Conceptual role and truth conditions', *Notre Dame Journal of Formal Logic*

—— (1985) 'Social content and psychological content', Colloquium in Philosophy, Oberlin College

MacDonald, C. with MacDonald, G. (1987) 'Mental causes and explanation of action', *Philosophical Quarterly* 36, no. 143

MacDonald, G. (1986) 'Modified methodological individualism', *Proceedings of the Aristotelian Society, Supplementary Volume*, 86

McDowell, J. (1978) 'Physicalism and primitive denotation', *Erkenntnis* 13

—— (1985) 'Functionalism and anomalous monism', in LePore & McLaughlin 1985

—— & Pettit, P. (1986) (edd.), *Subject Thought and Context*, Oxford: OUP

McGinn, C. (1978) 'Mental states, natural kinds and psycho-physical laws', *Proceedings of the Aristotelian Society*

—— (1980) 'Philosophical materialism', *Synthese* 44

—— (1982) 'The structure of content', Woodfield 1982

Mackie, J. (1973) *The Cement of the Universe*, Oxford: Clarendon Press

Margalit, A. (ed.) (1979) *Meaning and Use*, Dordrecht: Reidel

Morton, A. (1975) 'Because he thought he had insulted him', *Journal of Philosophy* 72

Nagel, E. (1961) *The Structure of Science*, London: Routledge

Oppenheim, P. & Putnam, H. (1958) 'The unity of science as a working hypothesis', in Feigl, Maxwell & Scriven 1958

Ortony, A (ed.) (1979) *Metaphor and Thought*, Cambridge: CUP

Papineau, D. (1985) 'Social facts and psychological facts' in Currie & Musgrove 1985

Peacocke, C (1979a) *Holistic Explanation*, Oxford: OUP

—— (1979b) 'Action and the ascription of content in propositional attitude psychology', Manuscript

—— (1981) 'Demonstrative thought and psychological explanation', *Synthese* 49

—— (1983) *Sense and Content*, Oxford: OUP

—— (1986) *Thought*, Oxford: Blackwell

Pears, D. (1975) 'The appropriate causation of intentional basic acts', *Critica* 7

170

Bibliography

—— (1984) *Motivated Irrationality*, Oxford: OUP

—— (1985) 'Intention and belief', in Vermazen & Hintikka 1985

Pettit, P. (ed.) (1986) *Subject, Thought, and Context*, Oxford: OUP

Putnam, H. (1975) *Mind, Language and Reality, Philosophical Papers*, Vol. 2, Cambridge: CUP

—— (1978) *Meaning and the Moral Sciences*, London: Routledge

—— (1981) *Reason, Truth and History*, Cambridge: CUP

—— (1983) *Realism and Reason: Philosophical Papers*, Vol. 3, Cambridge: CUP

—— (1988) *Representation and Reality*, Cambridge Mass: MIT Press

Russell, B. (1956) 'On denoting', *Logic and Knowledge*, ed. R. Marsh, London: Allen and Unwin

Sacks, O. (1976) *Awakenings*, London: Pelican

Searle (1983) *Intentionality*, Cambridge: CUP

—— (1985) *Minds, Brains and Science*, Cambridge Mass: Harvard UP

Stich, S. (1983) *From Folk Psychology to Cognitive Science: the case against belief*, Cambridge Mass: MIT/Bradford Books

Vermazen, B. & Hintikka, M. (edd.) (1985) *Essays on Davidson: actions and events*, Oxford: OUP

Watson, G. (1982) *Free Will*, Oxford: OUP

Woodfield, A. (1982) *Thought and Object*, Oxford: OUP

171

Index

172